Milldust and Roses
Memoirs

Larry Smith

For Jim —
Best wishes
to a long life

Larry

The Writer's Voice
Ridgeway Press

Cover photo by
James Jeffrey Higgins
(See his *Images of the Rust Belt*, KSU Press)
Cover layout by
Susanna Schwacke

Acknowledgments

We thank the following publications where some of these works
first appeared, sometimes in varied form.

*Asheville Poetry Review, Crooked River Press, Descant, Grand Lake Review,
The Heartlands Today, The Jawbone Book: 2001, The Journal, New Waves,
Ohio Magazine, Pine Mountain Sand & Gravel: Contemporary Appalachian
Writing, Red Brick Review, River-wind, River Teeth, Split W*sky, Whetstone,*
also writings in *I Have My Own Song for It: Modern Poems of Ohio* (Akron
University Press), *Scissors, Paper, Rock* (Cleveland State University
Poetry Center), and *Prayers to Protest* (Pudding House Press), and in
these books from Bottom Dog Press: *In Buckeye Country, The
Coffeehouse Poetry Anthology, Brooding the Heartlands, Beyond Rust,* and *Ohio
Zen.*

My thanks to the Ohio Arts Council for a Writing Fellowship and to
Bowling Green State University at Firelands College for a faculty
development leave, and to the generous readers at The Firelands
Writing Center of Firelands College.
Thanks also to M. L. Liebler and Mary Ann Wehler of The Writer's
Voice for all of their support, and to Allen Frost, David Budbill, and
Holly Beye for their advice and sharing.

Table of Contents

Part Two

Part Three

Season of Cancer

The dust rose from the mills and fell on everything,
including the rose bushes thriving along the fence.

Preface to Milldust and Roses

Mine is a common life, yet one that can be shared. One of my spiritual fathers, Henry David Thoreau, asks of every writer "a simple and sincere account of his life." I attempt to give that here. If our message lies in our intention, my hope in telling my life is to confirm the lives of others.

This story is measured in moments of recognition, mine and hopefully yours, through storytelling, that gift that exists to be given. My struggle to find this book's purpose was answered one day by recalling my father's basic belief in the value and dignity of each person, his mother's gift of gentle caring, and my own mother's love of language and play. It's a story in fragments, bits broken off or fallen to earth, shaped in memory yet refusing the too easy patterns of narrative coherence. I would not let the storytelling urge make a liar of me. And so the path lies broken before us, linked only by our human trust and our good intention to know and share a life. I have described it as fully as memory and understanding would allow.

I was born into a working-class family of the Ohio Valley, a war baby and child of the forties; I spent my growing-up years in the fifties, went from being a student to a husband and teacher in the sixties, became a pacifist and father in the seventies, and a writer and teacher in the eighties, nineties, and into this new millennium. And yet, this bare outline reveals little except my need to witness more fully here.

A few things I know: that my father's people came to the Ohio Valley from the farms of southern and central Ohio. That they were hard working Germans (humble and silent) and shanty-Irish (stubborn and sly). My mother's people came from a Scotch-Irish miner and Irish matron who settled near Pittsburgh and whose sons and daughters became professional men and witty wives. Mom's father was English from around Syracuse, New York. Somehow her mother got it into her head that they were better than the Smith's. It was a conflict the Smith's ignored, as my father proved himself an able provider by working in the mill with Mom's father. Unfortunately none of my people were much better at storytelling than I, though many could tell a good joke.

I know too that our little family grew up "working class poor," just making the rent and counting the pennies for school milk money. Yet Dad worked a job and a half most of his life. My wife's father earned less than mine, yet she was never *poor*, because she never heard the kitchen whispers and calls, the worries and threats put into words. My older brother and I, and my two younger sisters, grew up in slightly different families and forgive each other our separate visions. I grant them their varied memories as I trust they grant me mine.

I know that my mother loved to hear the songs of Perry Como and my father was fond of Eartha Kitt, and that they both liked to dance and made love more than the requisite four times. Though my mother bought a jar of white-out in 1980 to "correct" their marriage license, we know that my brother had been the cause of Mom's being a secret high school bride. It happens. Yet it may have also been cause for my father's abandoning his hopes of college until his boys came along. Mom never worked, except at the polls on election days, and was fine with that. She was often an inspired cook, and at other times a kitchen renegade, causing me to doubt my meals all my life (though I know I should get over it). Mom was an adequate housekeeper and a funny and caring mother, a friend to our many friends. She knew how to have and make fun.

Our small town lives were played out amidst the roar and smoke of the mills, in the nearby woods, in musty schoolrooms, old churches, on sunny playgrounds, under the street lights, and finally in the back seats of cars. Though we moved several times during my youth, Dad's railroading work was steady, and we kept our school friends until soon after college began. That, then marriage, became our first real moving away from home and launches the second part of this common life.

I followed my brother David to college because I knew I must—it was the freshly beaten path. Yet when I got there, I lacked any sense of why or wherefore. I was simply at college...Muskingum

College in little New Concord, Ohio; a Presbyterian college where I would begin to lose my religion and discover the world of ideas and art. Thus I made choices and checked the boxes: Math Major, Secondary Education. I found life in a dorm room interesting...crazy and lonely. I knew no one, and my roommate was majoring in playing cards down the hallway. And so my ties with back home were maintained by a daily letter writing to my girlfriend Barbara who was living at home and couldn't maintain the pace of the correspondence. I began working in the college cafeteria to be less of a financial burden and began making friends with fellow dishwashers. My romance with math soon faded in the boredom of Calculus 101, and a new one blossomed for writing and literature. We read the classics (Homer, Shakespeare, Dante) and wrote about them. I had found a world I would never leave again, one that dealt with life through its emotions and senses, its insights and knowings.

What accented my sense of alienation at college was the feeling of denial I felt there for my background—my working-class reality which this liberal arts culture ignored or treated with gloves. Not only was I struggling to find a place, I found my own world did not exist or belong there. Every other weekend I would hitch a ride back home, and when my folks drove me back on Sunday afternoons, it was painful to see them in this foreign land. I studied hard to show everyone that I belonged and that I would not waste my parents' second mortgage money. What the college did not realize, of course, was that they were providing me with the tools to one day write my life into the larger world.

Near the end of my junior year, my sweetheart handed me my high school ring and college pin, and I fell into that abyss I'd been reading about....listening to sad songs and licking the wounds of my own despair. She and I were a couple; we had a plan. Four months later, when I burned her love letters (and photos) in the back yard, I rose from the ashes. That summer I worked as a laborer at Weirton Steel, alongside of my railroading father, and I began hometown dating. Eventually I found the backyard rose of my wife Ann, the young girl I had watched playing in the alley, the cousin of my high school buddy, the student nurse at Wheeling living a block away.

A year later, when we both graduated in 1965, we took our marriage vows and summer jobs living in a makeshift apartment in Steubenville, then on to Euclid, Ohio, where I began high school teaching, and she started nursing at Euclid-Glenville Hospital. It was a long way from home, and we returned often, yet we grew our legs living along the lake. Three years later, with our baby daughter, Laura, we headed back to graduate school at Kent State University. Those Vietnam War years I worked part-time as a teaching fellow and Ann worked full-time at Robinson Memorial Hospital where they took the bodies of our students shot at Kent State. We grieved deeply and were forever changed, even as we moved on to my teaching at Firelands College along the lake in Huron, Ohio. Here the teaching and the standing up to war mixed, especially as the veterans returned and began to tell us stories in the classroom. Our son Brian was born in 1972 amidst new friendships and political campaigns. Ann was carrying him while canvassing for George McGovern. Her tears were deep when Nixon won; as were those of our friends. We grieved again and took long walks along the lake. In 1975 we moved a block away into a larger house where we welcomed the birth of our love-child Suzanne.

This large period of teaching, fathering, and beginning to write and publish my works and those of others was joined by Ann's getting one nursing degree after another. Friends came and went; we held them close and kissed them goodbye. Like good parents, we followed our children through school, eventually taking them to Sicily on a Fulbright Teaching Lectureship in 1980-1981, a year of adventure and intense bonding we would never trade. In 1988 and 1989 I returned to the Ohio Valley with my good buddy Tom Koba to produce two video programs to honor native poets James Wright and Kenneth Patchen and to pay homage to a way of life among the mill communities. Inevitably Ann and I came to know the loss of parents...Ann's father, both of mine...the birth of grandchildren, the way life keeps teaching us with blessings and losses–the growth it and we can bring together. I recall the last conversation I had with my mother as I walked her to my car. I open the door and she smiles, saying, "You're a good boy, you know?" I nod the say, "But, Mom, I'm a 48 year old man who's losing his hair." She slides in still smiling, and I walk around the car knowing that this self-realization will remain forever my own.

Part Three begins in the midst of all this...with my diagnosis of cancer in the fall of 1998, what I've called my "Cancer Season" here, that dark night from which light emerges. By March my prostate cancer was treated with radiation seeds in Seattle. Two years later, like the passengers of the jet liner that crashed in the fields of Sioux City, I too rose from the dead to face my life again in the cornfields. I know this too: that I have taken many spiritual paths toward growth as a person, sat and walked in meditation, read a thousand good books, taught my way through a thousand classes, ten thousand faces, toward some meaning. I have watched my children grow into caring adults with mates of their own, known the joy and pain of friendships, the dearness of family, the satisfaction of doing a few good works and seeing a few published and thus shared. With Ann as my life companion, we care for our garden. Retirement rises like a new kite on the horizon, where I watch ready to learn from the next wind. Though my life may seem common, I must confide, I have never found it dull.

Part One

(Photo ©   Larry Smith)

I remember you could put daisies
On the windowsill at night and in
The morning they'd be so covered with soot
You couldn't tell what they were anymore.

-Kenneth Patchen, "The Orange Bears"

AWAKENING

Soft sounds of people I love, a warm light come into my room. That is all, and yes, a sense of being alive to it, of knowing this is my life. I remember it now as a real dream.

I am a child of two, waking in my crib. There are my mother, a cheery, round-faced woman who sings to me, my father who smells strong holding me in his rough hands, and my brother who stares at me still and plays me into his games.

I was born into this working-class family in 1943, a war baby whose father was kept home from the war by a football injury (popped veins from a badly set collar bone). Each day he carries home his metal lunch pail. On the porch stoop, he stops to sit with his boys, sometimes opening it to peel a piece of fruit which he shares with us as we sit beside his tired legs. He is a railroader, and though he came to be other things to us—scout leader, teacher, friend—he is always this, a railroader in the steel mills that boom and roar at the foot of our Ohio Valley hills.

Every place looks down into the mills that run along both sides of that wide river. In first grade I would look out the window to the monstrous red towers of blast furnaces breaking the skies and looking most like huge swollen bombs that had somehow not gone off.

Wartime (and I would come to know many) does strange things to you, even when you are at home, a home veteran. Uncle Harry was the one off to war in the Philippines, so we kept track of him by letter and radio. Dad's sister, Aunt Mary, was a secretary in Washington D.C., but for the rest of us, war was a distant dream, a game we played with tiny soldiers, or by chasing each other with sticks used as rifles and bayonets.

Then there were those times when our parents grew strangely quiet before the radio, straining to hear the evening news. It seems my mother always had that radio going, singing along as we played on the hardwood floors, our legs thrown out behind us, the sun flecks floating down from the windows.

A sepia of old photos colors that time, not black or white or gray, but the deep red-brown of the mills and the war.

EARLY MOVES

Mingo Junction, Ohio [1943-1947]

Sunshine washing the front steps of our old apartment block the orange brick, two-stories at the crest of North Hill. From there you could see the town, the mills, that big Ohio River, the Appalachian foothills of West Virginia.

My brother and I would play with Joy and Betsy, war babies all of us, on the black steps of the fire escapes, our mothers inside cooking or cleaning and talking, our fathers at work in the mills or fast asleep inside, the bedroom door always kept closed.

Florence, Pennsylvania [1947-1949]

Open fields with big-eyed cows, gardens with bright flowers, my mother's parents living upstairs. It was a deal, my parents putting up $500 toward the down payment on the big, old farmhouse in the country—sharing the mortgage payments with Grandpa and Grandma Putnam. For my brother and me, it was rope swings Grandpa rigged on huge maple trees, a yard full of Grandma's flowers, an old barn full of tools kept locked, wild fields to roam, pathways leading back into dark woods.

For the men it was a long drive together to the Weirton mills, and lots of grass and weeds to mow when they came home. For the women it was the loneliness of being together all day. Grandma full of advice, Mother full of doubts and fears. Even a child knows the sound of tears through a bedroom door.

And then my brother went off to school, leaving me alone all day, inside leafing through magazines and listening to music and mother in the kitchen. It was playing 'cars' on the back porch, talking to the neighbor's cows, tossing them apples, watching them make wet plops in the field, or lying on the front porch swing and falling asleep thinking of the games we could play when David got home.

We couldn't have a dog, though Grandma had her canaries. She was always scolding us for our ways. Once I surprised her from behind a door, and she screamed, "You terrible, sneaky child! You're just like your mother." When I told mother that, she ran off to her room. When Father came home, I heard her telling him, "She loves those birds more than our boys." And Father, "Well, maybe for her, that's a start."

We could only venture upstairs to use the bathroom, pee in the toilet where Grandpa dumped out his pipe. We shouldn't flush; we had a cistern. I learned to plop my turds through Grandpa's circles of floating tobacco. And there were the long silences of Sunday meals up there. Something wasn't working. Everyone knew.

There was not enough room in one house, though there were plenty of rooms. When sister Janis was born, we began packing. My brother and I packed our comic books, our toy trucks and brown bears, and rode inside the cab of a pick-up truck my Uncle Harry drove. At the red light at the edge of town, I could see Mom and Dad with baby Janis, singing in our car.

Mingo Junction, Ohio (520 Murdock Street) [1949-1954]

We moved into a thin, three-story, wooden frame house two blocks from where Grandma Smith and Uncle Harry lived. We called it 'Uncle Mont's House' because we paid him the $40 rent each month. There were houses all around, the hoot and clatter of the trains, the smell and taste of mill in the air. We ate it without question.

It was running in the alley with friends, walking to school each day, making things from the wood that Dad cut for us. It was watching my sister suck the dirt from stones in the yard, her sweet baby laughter. It was sleeping in my own bed, hearing my brother breathe in the little room. It was Mother smiling on our toast. It was home.

Mingo Junction, Ohio (310 Murdock Street) [1954-1965]

Mother wanted a better house, the one Grandma Smith rented to an older couple. Father said, "Let it lie, woman. We're okay where we are." She didn't let it lie. She wrote, then called them; then wrote and called them again. Three months later they moved on and we into the family house we kept for decades. It was a bigger wooden frame place with a back porch and yard. It was a house away from her mother. Soon Dad's sister, Aunt Bay, moved home from Washington, D. C. with our new Uncle Ray.

Mom had baby Deborah; Bay had cousin Jeff. For decades we were a family; we were a tribe.

310 MURDOCK STREET

Long I lived in that green river valley along the burnt edge of the mills and railroad, knew the lights through unwashed panes at every hour, the sounds of trains clashing and sirens punctuating the industrial roar, and at night the trucks shifting down through our lives, headlights moving a pale scrim across the ceiling cracks. Voices downstairs were working things out while we kids slept through the poverty of getting by. The winter wind slipped under the sill while my clock radio played on the small table before I slept, my right arm above my head tricking the sleep on, waking to the cold of a coal furnace, the bathroom floor a chill of linoleum and steam rising slowly from the sink where I washed the new day into my face, the kitchen where we ate and talked under the dropped ceiling tile passing the toast to hands, emptying cereal boxes, the television voices already selling the day to Mom in the other room. All of us went off to schools of some kind, leaving behind the old life of closets and attic, basement tools, our faces held in mirrors and photos, our parents moving slowly through amber.

THE GATHERING, FAMILY PHOTO, OHIO 1932

At the Smith family farm in Vinton County, Ohio, the brothers stand out on the county road where they have parked their Model-T's. Mont and Ernie, Bundy, Murray, and Wilmer, all in shirt-sleeves, trading talk about crops and weather and cars. The younger men lean on trees or sit on running boards listening. Not known for their story telling, the Smiths nevertheless can talk or hold a silence till it speaks. Someone spots a hawk and they all stand silent staring above the trees, waiting to catch a sight.

The women are inside baking pies or setting tables in the back yard while the girls drink iced tea on the front porch whispering as their mothers talk of other days, of the church revival meetings of who was saved and who was not.

Not real smokers or drinkers, the Smiths are farmers mostly, and their faces say, "That's how she is—Don't ask me twice."

And this is how they look, as Mildred brings out the new Kodak and snaps them standing in straw hats and shirt sleeves, just before someone calls, "Supper."

GRANDMA SMITH

My grandmother Smith couldn't speak with words—anymore than baby sister Janis. And I'd heard how Uncle Harry now changed Grandma when she lost control of herself. Her eyes were as big as mine and just as brown when I slept beside her, hearing her breath and the Old Ben alarm clock ticking across her little room. My brother would be sleeping on the couch or with Uncle Harry. I never felt Grandma rise, never watched her dress at the foot of the bed, but there she would be at the kitchen stove in morning light turning eggs over easy, toasting bread a side at a time. And when it was just she and I, she would sit at the table and watch me eat.

We were living then with my mother's mother in Pennsylvania, so I only visited on weekends or if my folks needed a night out. The baby would be left with my other grandmother, the one who talked all the time. "Please," I would beg, "can I stay with Grandma Smith and Uncle Harry." Mother would be standing in her slip, brushing her long dark hair before a mirror. "Please, can I, Mom?"

And she would turn and say, "Go ask your father. It's he who'll have to drive you over there."

So I would go help him look for his dress shoes, the black ones with the wing tips. "Here they are," I'd call, "down here under the bed." And I would stand and watch his big work hands make knots out of the shoe strings, the way he'd taught me, and I would ask again, "Can I please stay with Grandma?" And he'd look up and not have to ask which one.

"Sure. She'd like that. Your brother and baby sister can stay here with Grandma Putnam."

We didn't have to call ahead and ask. We'd just show up at their front door, knock and go in, and they'd welcome us. Uncle Harry would be listening to the Indians' ball game, keeping score on the lines he'd drawn on brown paper. Dad would go back to Mom in the car, and Grandma would rise from her rocker. She would lead me back into the kitchen where the light would come on, and a row of pies would appear on the table. I usually picked apple because I had seen her quick hands pare and core them, unwrapping their skin like a ribbon to the floor. So I would sit and eat amidst her gentle humming. The crust was as white as her skin.

*   *   *

By the time baby Janis began to talk and we were living next to them in Mingo, Grandma had begun to walk off. She would be in the yard hanging up sheets one minute and gone down the street the next. When I was there, I'd go after her. Uncle Harry would come into the house and announce, "Well, she's gone," and I'd set down my toy soldiers or stop exploring the basement dark with its wonderful spiders, and I'd be gone after her.

I would start off asking "Now, where would she go?" When that didn't help, I'd think again, "Okay, now if I were Grandma, where would I be now?" Best of all was just to go where I wanted to and find Grandma there too. It was a small town near the railroad tracks, so sometimes I'd go down there, just in case she was remembering Grandpa. He'd been killed by a train while working in the steel mill. I was only two at the time, so mostly I'd heard about it from Mother. Grandma could talk back then, and so when the mill offered a compensation—to pay her $1000 or $100 a year for the rest of her life, she looked around her house at the faces of her sons and Aunt Bay, and she'd said, "With this family here, I'll be needing something for the long haul." That's what Mother told me she said, "for the long haul."

I was down around the tracks when I saw Grandma on the sidewalk by the underpass. She was walking fast and still had her apron over her house dress, so it looked like maybe she was just running to a friend's, or chasing a kid who'd run off. When I caught up to her at the traffic light before the Mill Bar, I just took her hand into mine. She looked down at me, a boy of seven with big brown eyes, and she said her first word in years; "Deb?" she said like a question. "Deb?" just that once, and then she turned back with me to climb the hill to home. I felt warm and important then; my father's name was Deb.

MY WORKING CLASS EDUCATION

FIRST

In first grade we lined up for everything. Saying the alphabet helped us know our place. I came near the end, I knew that, though I didn't know why. What was order to a kid of five? My memory was a seed garden growing each day as I fed it graham crackers and milk. There was my Roy Rogers pencil box that I forgot at school till someone kept it with its sliding drawer and the good smell of erasers.

So we lined up for everything, like I said—music and gym, lunch and recess, getting on our coats to go home. And one time we stood along the steps at the nurse's office to stand at her lap as she ran a piece of dry spaghetti through our hair. We just didn't ask.

SECOND

Mrs. Reisling spoke to us soft. She was small but we listened to each word—like spiders dancing over waters, coins pressed into our hands. She smelled of flowers in rain when she touched us with our names.

I remember one day seeing myself in the window as I stood at the back sharpening my pencil. She was watching me. I was someone too. I would do good work, lay things out straight, clean up after myself without asking.

THIRD

My third grade teacher, Mrs. Brettel, was my mother's friend, but I was not her child.

She was the one who taught me to love birds, feeding us drawings of them to color each Thursday after gym. These were the birds I watched around our yard each morning and night. And I would rub and rub those crayons into each bird's pale skin till it felt warm and sticky like blood.

I remember how we couldn't believe Mrs. Brettel had a son and a daughter, even though she told us of them. We thought they were story book kids. Then one day she brought the boy to class because he was too sick to go to school and too young to stay home alone. He sat at my desk with me, a quiet brother.

FOURTH

She held my hand as we marched around the gym floor, and her hand wasn't cold or wet like the others, but warm in a way that made me sing inside. Her dress brushed my fingers and I felt myself turn like a bird flying through the sun.

When she moved away, I vanished too. I was a fish without air, a poem without words.

FIFTH

I was taken in by the twins. After all, there were two of them, and they danced together for my birthday party. "First you put your two knees/ close up tight..." Only there were four knees, not two, doubling my delight as they tapped and shuffled, kicked and turned on our linoleum floor. "Could-she love, could-she woo, could-she, could-she, could-she coo!" It was years before I knew those were words and not just sounds of a flirting girl.

My mother baked a huge cake, in the shape of a fire truck, but we fed all the kids cupcakes thick with sugared icing.

SIXTH

Shirley said I was too young to kiss her deeply. I'd seen it in a movie once. This was a game we were playing at a birthday party, going into the other room alone together.

Outside I could hear the trains, and I stood near her holding hands in the dark light of the window. I put my hand in the small of her back as she leaned into my face. Her lips were smooth as rain.

SEVENTH

We threw the basketball so long our arms grew warm. Then we ran rings around the point dribbling till we passed, pivoting into the nest. We loved the ball loving us. Five of us on a side, the coach commanding all of us to share the ball, drive into the net, get back on defense. It made such sense. We gave our lives to it.

EIGHTH

On the blackboard the teacher wrote the names. *Honor Role* it said, and I was never up there, never one of the chalked ones, due to be erased in six weeks. I was busy studying the way girls' necks looked in the window light as they reached up to pull the blinds, the soft sway of skirts up the aisle, the warm smell of lilacs, the thin hair on their arms, the transparence of skin across their wrists.

I studied enough to get by, not too much to become unpopular. My locker held my books at night as I burst out the door— eager to drop my innocence, holding strong to my ignorance.

NINTH

I fell in love with unreality in the semi-dark of the movie house, then on the steps before school—where the girls stood before the brick, like sibyls and sirens mesmerizing my heart.

And so I bought an old guitar with my newspaper money, wore my finger tips to callouses over bone, sliding them up and down the long neck till the chords cried out and fell like rain over the town. It was my own blood pulse I heard behind the notes climbing into space then falling over everything. And I raced through records following the sound down streets, running it back through strings and wood, vibrating it through my legs and arms, biting off notes, releasing others, pounding the strings like drums, over my own little town.

TENTH

I loved reading as a kid; then like an oaf, I'd misplaced it for running the streets and rock and roll music. I found it again in book report choices...*Huck Finn* by Mark Twain, *Main Street* by Sinclair Lewis, *Winesburg, Ohio* by Sherwood Anderson—I didn't know there could be books like these.

So in my head whole worlds began to breathe. I'd watch people at the stadium, in the theater, on the buses, and their lives would cross over into mine. When they got off, I'd continue with them up the hill and into the houses of their lives.

I began to write it down. It was like learning to dance for the first time or watching a film at a drive-in where the movie plays while the lives go on inside each car, and all you had to do was listen close inside yourself.

I didn't tell this to anyone.

ELEVENTH

The coal truck backed over the curb and into our house. He said he was turning his rig around to unload. Mother cried at the cracked plaster and glass all over the living room rug, and father hadn't even been told yet.

I knew this would make the papers that night, "Truck Backs Into House." We lived in a small town. Soon it would all be cleaned up and fixed, but forever people would speak of it, *the house with the truck in it.*

At school the next day I was a hero or something, and for what? I wasn't even there when the back gate came loose and dumped a load of coal into the yard. But I did help shovel it into the face of the coal shoot for hours when Dad came home and made the deal—the coal was free, and $100 for the broken house. That was the short of it.

The long of it was my mother's fear of ever leaving the house alone again. Someone always had to be home to welcome such things.

TWELFTH

We were playing euchre down in Ken's family room. The record player was chanting, "Take a Message to Mary" and in the chorus, we all looked up to sing. "Take a message to Mary.../ but don't tell her where I am."

I was in love with Barbara then, fair faced and pony-tailed, with a brain that ran like a train. She helped me with my civics and biology; I helped her with math and English. We stood at each other's locker before and after school.

When Barbara told me she was going to college someday, it sounded like a place to visit. I had a brother off at college in Tennessee then. *But what does that mean—college? Where?* She didn't answer, but looked up slowly from her book with sad eyes asking, *What about you? What will you do with yourself after you graduate?* I saw two roads before me: one down the hill and into the mills, and the other out the highway and on to college.

That night as I watched my friends laying down their cards one by one in silence, I started adding up the points. And I asked myself, *What will I do with myself?* Slowly I began counting backwards all the way to one.

SOME STORIES OF POVERTY

I waken from a sleep troubled but unable to remember anything. It is just a winter day full of holes and shadows, and I am already late.

*   *   *

I am eating my lunch outside on the school steps, and it is snowing. I reach into my sack. I pull out one wet cabbage roll. I have no fork or spoon, and so I give it to the boy standing at my feet. He begins to eat it like a pear. The sparrows in the bushes descend on him and devour it. He looks back at me. A shadow on the steps—my face in the window.

*   *   *

I sleep, I dream. A girl at the school fountain speaks to me. She is standing in her slip and socks, and I am in love with her voice. When she turns, I can see the large holes in her back as if she has been beaten with a broken dish. The water leaks out onto the tile floor, and I try to soak it up with my shirt.

*   *   *

We boys are being shoved into line, then led into the gymnasium locker room. It is the first time, and the smells are old and new. We are all told to undress, put on our tennis shoes and shorts. I look around. So many stand motionless, shadows waiting. Someone shouts and they take off their shoes and socks. Their feet are painted with dirt, but they do not rub it off. We all stand in the gray silence of it. Another whistle sends us running out, yelling from our lungs, echoing into the huge and empty coldness of the room. Our feet pound the dark wooden floors as we run along the padded walls. We throw balls at each other; we forget our names and clothes. Another whistle and we run back into the locker room where the showers call us. I am among the few who strip naked and enter. The others sit and watch. When I return, wet towel wrapped around my bare ass, I see. The others are shadows again, seated along the walls, lacing shoes. I look down at the ring of blood circling my waist.

*   *   *

My mother is putting our fruit into a box. There are oranges and bananas and pears. My hand is pushed away. "This isn't for you," she says. "It's for the sick girl next door." And I go out onto the back porch and curse. My hunger is being fed with stones. I look through the dusky air at her little yard. I see—the yard is barren and all the plants are bent and dying in the cold. Mother whispers to me through the screen: "The father has left them. They have no food." It is as sharp as truth, as solemn as prayer. I sit on the silent stair. A river runs through me. I drink the empty air.

DAYS OF SUN AND POLIO

That day, we marched down to the Nurse's Office, then stood in a line along the tall and echoey hallway watching the faces of the others come out, reading the letters of pain in their eyes. And our teachers would shush us all with the word "Polio."

It was 1953, the year the Cleveland Indians had gone far, and we too had ridden the Little League bus all the way to Municipal Stadium where we stood in rows to pee, then walked out to our seats in the lower deck. And when Al Rosen smacked a hard line drive down the third base line, we all rose and ran madly towards the ball.

As the polio line inched inside the office, we could see Dr. Riney through glass bending towards the kid's white arm with his long needle, and the nurse whispering, "It's okay, Honey. This will keep you well. Look away."

On television at night we might see again some kid in an "iron lung" machine, helping him to breathe. Its huge metal holding him, its accordian lung pumping more air. All that long summer we did not swim at the public pool nor try to kiss the girls in the alley.

We acted strong but wanted our mother's arms around us, as we did when the bomb-drill alerts went off, screaming us out into the hallways again, where we would lean our heads onto our arms against the cold metal lockers, waiting and thinking, "The Russians are coming to bomb us to hell and gone." Words of the older kids out on the playground, stones they had picked up and thrown.

Sure, there were the faces of girls out in the sunlight, the soft touch of their hands as we called someone over. And there were teachers' hands too on our shoulders as we fit our letters between the lines. Our joys came like a snowfall one day, and the next were covered with ashes.

Then one day my friend Billy could not come to school, and the next, and the next, till finally we heard the words: "Polio Myelitis...Infantile Paralysis," from our mother's lips as they quickly turned away. For Billy the shots were too late, and so our fathers showed us again how to wash our hands at the sink. I stood there staring down through water to the soap bar at the bottom of the bowl, and I thought of Billy's legs lying limp on his bed.

I could not connect it all then either. But I knew it like my worn blue jacket hanging there in school closet waiting for me to wear it home.

THE SILENCE OF TOOLS

My father worked in basement silence, bent like a crane over his workbench, tools in hand, thinking his way through with them, connecting cause and effect til there was no room left for fault or waste. Near him stood the coal furnace he kept, the coal on the floor, three footsteps away.

And I sat on the steps beneath the hanging light watching his hands, straining for him to be set free, to come back upstairs with mother and me, sit on the back porch together as the mill roared softly by the river.

But no, he seemed to love it there below in that silence he harvested from tools. And I would go up to my room and swim alone through lost rivers of words.

BINGO NIGHT AT THE MINGO SHOW

There was a time when I just about *lived* at the Mingo Show, soaking up the soft matinee light as the screen glowed with the real dreams of cowboys and show girls, gangsters and gun molls, comics and heroes, or the semi-sweet tales of Disney animals or loving families that touched and informed my life. Now we can all catch most of these old films on the American Movie Classics channel or colorized on Ted Turner's Network Television, or we can go out to the plaza and rent them for our home video cassette recorders. But you and I both know it won't be the same. The actors and story will be there, but the light from the television won't be as bright, and it won't reflect onto the warm upturned faces of the people of our hometown, the real communal legacy we had in our hometown movie houses. For, more than our stadiums and gymnasiums, our churches and schools, our movie houses were our community fountains where we all met and drank a common culture.

Each small town had one as I discovered one day in 1970 while standing in the hardware store in Huron. I was looking around at the long layout of the building when someone explained it had once been the town movie house. Eating lunch at the Star Café in downtown Sandusky, I looked up from my chicken noodle soup to the ceiling and old projectionist window still open. The larger towns had several. It was a mark of our independence when a group of friends could ride the bus (another cultural carrier) to Steubenville to share lunch and a first run film. There we could choose between The Capitol, The Grand, or the Paramount Theatres—even the names taught us something about style, as did the marbled urinals in the restroom, the dark ruby curtains, the white shirts and bow ties of the ushers. In the lush darkness we could all escape the glare and blare of our milltowns, try on the clothes of movie life, and return to our streets somehow wiser.

Fourteen cents was the ticket price for years at the Mingo Show, till they finally upped it to a dime and a nickel. So, we took back pop bottles, ran errands for neighbors, and went to the movies often.

On Friday and Saturday *High Noon* might be showing, and on Sunday, Monday, and Tuesday *The Quiet Man* would play. In the middle of the week, on Wednesday and Thursday, you could catch a showing of *A Streetcar Named Desire*. The lives on the screen seemed to extend our own as stretched into the fresh anguish of Marlon Brando or James Dean. We packed it in together at the OK Corral with Burt Lancaster and Kirk Douglas. For working-class kids, we traveled a lot in our own hometowns.

Sometimes, if I had done my homework and if Grandma was going so that Mom had no sitter, I could go along for the midweek showing of a film like *Born Yesterday*. It would be dish and bingo night, and the lights would be on as the usher (some friend's older brother, or a kid who had graduated from his paper route) would hand us our gravy boats which Mom and Grandma would cradle on their laps beside me.

On bingo night after the first showing, the lights would come on. We could all suddenly see each other. The place would be packed with smiling neighbors and kids rubbing the sleep from their eyes. "Mingo Mike" Kendrach, the manager, would come out onto the stage with a couple of grinning ushers rolling in the bingo board and balls. He would tap the microphone a couple times and ask, "Is this on?" To which we would all shout back, "No, it's on!" and roar with laughter. Then he would smile and declare, "Good evening, everyone. And welcome to the Mingo Show." It seems now that the general response to this was a kind of relieved laughter. Then Mike would get serious as he announced, "Tonight, ladies and gentlemen, there will be fifty numbers called in our game. And I remind you that tonight's grand prize is . . ." (There was silence here, just to be certain we knew the stakes.) " . . . 200 dollars!" Real sighs went up at the sound of the amount, for most of us had already spent it in our heads buying new refrigerators and bikes. Of course, this was before our state lotteries made winning outrageous amounts seem almost common. "Yes, 200 dollars is tonight's prize," Mingo Mike would declare, and I could watch my mom holding her card as she smiled down on me, as if to say, "Boy, wouldn't your father be surprised."

I remember that a girl I liked in high school once won the jackpot amidst a cheering crowd. She got to go down front as they read off her card and pronounced her "Tonight's winner." She turned her $200 into a set of caps for her front teeth and became so famous that people would stop on the street just to point her out. "See her, she's the girl that won the Bingo jackpot at the show." Such downright glamour in a small town.

Another time, when my brother was off in college, I watched as his best friend won the coverall jackpot for $100 and $50 worth of merchant coupons—a free haircut at Toni's, shoe repair at Arman's, sundae at Isly's, $10 tool at Gilchrest Lumber, pool game at Dugan's. As fate had arranged, it was the night before he shipped out in the Navy, so he never got to collect.

Mingo Mike would begin by reminding us to take the free space on our card (only those who payed adult prices received cards), and he would begin the reading of the balls handed to him by the smiling usher from a guest drawer. About 10 balls in he would caution us, "Remember, this is a *cover-all* game. All spaces must be covered in order to win." But we were still young into the game, and the odds seemed about right. Later, when he announced, "Ladies and gentlemen, we have only five numbers left," you could hear a bridge of sighs stretch across the audience–a sympathetic acceptance of our mutual fate.

Usually there were no grand winners, but always we each had won. We had shared the common experience of America—in the film and in each other. I carry lots of those old films within me—their human themes and gestures. I also still carry the warm faces of the people I lived with—my neighbors and friends, even my enemies and their moms, the folks from North Hill, Resevoir Hill, Church Hill, and the Bottom: the old women behind us who chattering in strange tongues—Slovak, Italian, Polish, Hungarian—their dark-eyed daughters sitting with their mustached beaus, my black friends nested in the back corner, my English teacher and her best friend. Whether in a melting pot or rich salad bowl of American life, the experience made us all human and together. And as we piled out of the theatre into the evening light, people smiled into each other's eyes as they joked about losing the grand prize—"And what would I do if I won—buy a new mink coat!" There was good cheer to spare. And as we walked out into the night, I would take the soft hands of my mother and grandmother, and we would climb together the streets of home.

RISE AND SHINE

For my father

First with a warm washcloth smelling ripe with Lifebuoy, then with a swallow of cold water tasting of iron, he tries to wake into the day. Outside the bathroom window he hears the cold cries of birds around the garbage cans dreaming of summer.

Opening our middle bedroom door he tramps lightly as he can across old carpet to closet where he lifts down his work pants. His wallet identity bulges in back pocket, and he tries not to shake the coins and keys as he leans, sliding one leg in then the other. And with just the nightlight on the floorboard he casts his slow eyes across his two boys still slumbering towards morning.

He does not wish a different life, only one where time allows that each may sit together eating warm oatmeal with brown sugar like she once made when they were young married. Yet he knows his destination, who he is, what the cost of milk and white bread are.

Descending steps now he wonders how much colder it will be in the mill yard where he works inside dark weather braking on the railroad half his life now.

Pays the bills, he thinks standing alone in kitchen light. In a few minutes he will lower his tea bag into the porcelain pan, wait two clock turns, then shovel three spoons of sugar and pour the steaming brew into his father's old green thermos.

Before he leaves he enters the cold basement smell of oil and laundry soap. In firelight stokes the coal furnace, leans into the job. Yet what he really wants is to shake the whole world awake break silence with his iron gong that each mother's son might come see what a father's life can be, what a father's life comes to.

BATHING WITH MEN

We drove out the old road—my dad, my brother, and me—out past the junk yard through the trees, past the hills that slid onto the road when it rained, beyond Devil's Den and First Bridge. The air was warm as Grandma's bread, and the dust rose from the road in clouds of sunlight.

My brother drove with his elbow out the window, Dad smiling at his side, finding a station on the radio. I rolled my t-shirt sleeves up like theirs, but when I'd look around, they'd come undone.

Dave took our old DeSoto around the bend, then up onto Second Bridge which rattled like a box of old coffee cans. And we'd stop there to watch the other boys in old shorts leap through air, past leaves, into the yellow-green stream below.

He turned us gently down the dirt road through weeds, past others standing by their cars, all of us nodding in evening sun. At the rocks, Dad said, "Good. Now ease it slow, son, just up to the back wheels."

We were giving our car a summer bath, and I remember leaving my shoes on the back seat floor, stepping out into a cold stream that pulled at my legs and feet. Dad would bring two buckets out from the trunk, and we'd begin emptying the stream onto our metal green car. One bucket after another as my father poured the sweet liquid onto roof and hood, we boys circling at his legs with wet heavy rags, rubbing ourselves into it.

I remember feeling a button then and seeing that the cloth I worked so hard in my hands was the dress of my little sister home with my mother. The sun was moving slow into the trees, the water tugging me forward, as I let go of the cloth's thin fingers, watching it float gently on the stream...

When I looked around, Dad was throwing my brother through the air into the middle of the laughing stream, and I cried hard, "Dad, please, Dad, do me. Do me next!"

RECLAIMING #1

We threw their basketball over the hill. Let them go search for it down in the weeds beside the creek. We had been whipped enough by their words in and out of school, so we snatched it out of their yard one night. Joey said it would be cool if the ball reached the creek and floated out into the river, orange rubber bobbing like a buoy to mark our feat. But I could see it lodged down there against a rock at the base of a locust tree. I remember thinking that some kid would come along and take it home, or maybe sensing its path, throw it out upon the waters.

*　　　*　　　*

I watched her standing at the hall fountain in her blue flowered dress talking with Rosemary DiCarlo. Her smooth blond hair around her cheeks took my breath, the way the wind can with a small child. I had taken a box of cough drops from the school store to give to her with the bluest eyes. In eighth period study hall she was all that kept me alive. And though she sat in the back along the windows, she was there in the room before my eyes. I followed her once up to the pencil sharpener, stood close inside her steps, smelling her soft hair in the afternoon sunlight. When she turned into my eyes, I swallowed hard my words, handed her the box of chewy cough drops, tasted her laughed surprise, then measured it against the steps she walked away.

*　　　*　　　*

I watched the history teacher cry again today, a man who had been principal once, made the fool of boys my age. I had seen so few men cry, I stared at him, all of us wondering further with our eyes. Was that the reason he stood in back so much, rolling his questions down the aisles like stray gutter balls no one even laughed at anymore? His shame and ours went up in smoke inside that little room. And I would turn toward the window, remembering my father shoveling soft coal into our furnace when he came home from work, mill dirt still written across his face and shirt, and all his tears locked inside a stone.

*　　　*　　　*

When I came home Uncle Ray was in our old garage. He was standing over his engine talking down to my dad who slid beneath the car on cardboard spread across the ground. There were the three of us there: I holding the light. Dad doing all the work. Ray telling me a joke my father never would, and on his breath the sour sweet smell of whiskey carrying the words into our laughter. There was no question whose boy I was.

*　　　*　　　*

I would walk home from Sunday school and find Mother drinking her cup of coffee before the television set. Dad would be sitting in church by then, beside his mother and my brother. He might lean over and ask David, "Where's your brother?" and get back just a shrug. For I would be sitting there on the couch watching Oral Roberts lay on his hands to *heal* the sick, tasting my mother's toast and drinking her soft laughter.

*　　　*　　　*

And there was Crazy Mary, woman of a dozen purses strung around her dirty neck, talking out loud to herself as she walked our streets. And from the other side we would hurl looks and words at her, "Crazy Mary, will you come out? Crazy Mary, will you come out?"

At times she would disappear and we would hear stories of her sitting somewhere in jail, or sighted in other towns down river, maybe walking the highways like a grackle in the snow. We knew she'd stolen the money out of the church votive box. My mother remembered her as a wild girl without a mother that the schools couldn't handle. We wove our own tales of her that melted when we saw her dirty face again, her coat of rags.

And when shadows crept across the pavement of our lives, till the streetlights came on, we would climb the hill into the weeds before her house and chant, "Crazy Mary, will you come out?" into the night. The wind blowing hard against our own wild hair and eyes.

*　　　*　　　*

When we walked out the road past the junkyard into the trees, it was not just to smoke or talk our dreams. We would find a small creek and walk up its banks snagging burrs and jiggers with our clothes, stopping to scoop up a salamander in our hands, sitting on a log smelling the bed of leaves.

These were the woods where my father had come to burry our dogs in among the violets, kneeling on the wet earth. And when I felt his tears beside me, it stopped my own, so I could breathe again. All that day I would see the dark stain on his pant knee as if it were blood.

We boys would bring back the strange colored stones held deep in our pockets, and the rough sticks we used as staffs. At the edge of sound, where the trains and traffic joined the roar of the mills. At the crest of the hill and the first street into town, we would turn back to face the long valley and cast out our sticks, watching them soar, float a moment, then fall through the trees to the waiting earth.

RECLAIMING #2

Crossing the tracks wasn't easy. It took speed and control and a certain wild flare for facing the diesel death bearing down upon you. If you relaxed too much, you could be swept up and gone into a story they'd tell of the kid who got smashed one day down on those tracks. First you had to duck off the road and step over the guardrail. Then you ran or slid down the bank balancing yourself by grasping onto the tall weeds. The rugged sumac greeted you along the bottom, their fuzzy pods blossoming wounds. The cool spring along the sidetracks might call to you, but even those empty gondola cars could suddenly jolt into life and death. Ultimately you had three sets of tracks to cross over, and they wound there along the bend before the mill. So you had to run for it, hard and blind, your feet barely touching ground.

That one time I stopped to call back to a friend, I heard the roar and looked up into the diesel face—stood frozen in life's long moment—then dove into the bushes and rocks on the other side. When the train had passed my friend's stricken face, I was already dusting myself off, trying to swallow my heart again, and ready to beg the biggest glass of water from Flora's Bar across the road.

*   *   *

My brother's friends were into music, the earliest rock-n-roll that 1950's radio stations would allow. Pittsburgh's WAMO would play Black rhythm and blues, a mean Bo Diddley chanting with drums as his guitar chords climbed into flames. The words wound like a dirty boogie love song just outside our white boy hearts. We bought the records, a player, and found places to sit and listen–at Hatcher's upstairs, Merzy's garage, our basement. I would watch the older guys listening with their eyes closed, as I sat tapping my foot, rocking, and dreaming my hands around a high school girl in my brother's class. She walked before me down the school hall, her dark hair swaying in the light, her skirt dancing, and as we reached the steps, she went down, and I fell over her, my face into her hair, grasping my arm around her smooth waist, lifting her into the laughter of our catching breath...

A new 45 record would click, then fall lightly onto the turntable. The arm would glide over and the needle set down deep into the grooves. It would be Gene Vincent crying for "Woman Love" or wailing "Be-Bop-A-Lula" into our wild pulsing hearts.

*   *   *

We walked up the hill together after the dance, the two of us holding hands in the cold air as the night Bessemer spread its pink glow over everything. I had been watching her all week, the soft swaying of her pony tail as she walked down the halls, the way she would hold her arm up in class each time the teacher asked, sometimes bracing it with her other hand, the way she leaned her back against her locker waiting for the first bell, her books pressed against her breasts. As I passed, she would smile without asking. If I could be this much a part of her, why couldn't I be more?

And so that night we held each other tight in the slow music dark of the wordless dance floor. Her hands were warm telegrams which I opened with my own, both of us letting our feet move us closer than we ever dreamed before, leaning together in the dark between songs, till all that was left was the climbing of the hill to her arms, the sweet taste of our lips in the light outside her house, the warm touch within.

*   *   *

I didn't know you had to go away to be treated for cancer. Then one day my grandfather just disappeared to the Hospital in Pittsburgh. It became a phrase spoken again and again when my father came home and asked ... *the Hospital in Pittsburgh* ...my mother saying it through tears as she stirred our soup. "Will you boys be alright here alone?" she'd ask, and we would nod into our food. There was not enough light to fill the house anymore. There was just enough food and water to drink.

Without asking, I would invite Barbara over to do our homework together on the couch. My brother would go upstairs to play his records loud enough for us to hear, and we would lay down our books and hold each other's life. We danced inside our arms, smelled the baking warm. A train whistle would enter our kiss. And then the front door came open and we stood up together, whispering with our eyes. The light came on and I read my father's face. "Your grandfather died this afternoon," he spoke too fast into the little room. I felt it going deep into my chest. And then my mother entered and there was not enough space to breathe.

RECLAIMING # 3

Opening the big blue dictionary and releasing all those words, letting the pages skate across my thumb—words ticking by me as they climbed. Mother spoke them to us at night from books. And I soon learned to string them together myself, to run them along in rows, making sentences sing through my brain. It was called reading and I learned to empty myself to it, to open and swallow books whole, hundreds of them, alone.

*   *   *

It was something Mother did. It came easy, the writing of rhymes. Saying them at parties, sending them on birthday cards. Though I would never see her write them, I would know her handwriting there on the page and love the wonder of her making. They were always funny, always turning to laughter what might have been love or sadness. And she showed me the ones her mother had written, folded in old letters, so much the same, yet sharper, Irish, more the old family wit that forced the women to dance without touching, without lifting the arms.

*   *   *

On Saturdays my brother would take me with him inside the town library, the old market shelves now filled with books, something you could get inside, something that could touch you, like the movie matinees we would enter those hot afternoons, our books cradled in our arms. On the screen were our heroes, Tarzan of the Jungle and Jungle Jim—thrilling us with feats of courage. And the stories of cowboys and ballplayers in slim yellow books I would read later in my bed, measuring my life with words.

*   *   *

I would be sent over to Grandmother's to practice my spelling with Uncle Harry. I was to compete in the Spelling Bee, and so we tried to drill into me the order of letters in words. It was fifth grade and already I knew I could not memorize, could not find the way to hold the letters or numbers in rows. They would come rolling out onto the ground like dropped marbles or stones.

And there were the words in poems we were forced to memorize, words I loved but could not hold right. My mind was a stutter that could not contain itself. So that I would climb into my bed at night through tears, dreading the standing before the class unclothed. I grew to hate the poems I once loved, lost their dance and turn and climb. And though I took the parts in plays, I did so knowing I could never hold the lines, would be sneaking the play book out of my pants and into my sweating palms just before I went on.

By sixth grade I had abandoned all poetry, when the teacher passed out those tiny ivory colored booklets for us to hold and actually keep. Our own book of poems, the close dance of sounds and rhymes, the mix and match of games, the building of pace through space. I read them over again and again till my head filled with them, till the words came out as lines building their way to the skies. Soon I was building mine.

RADIO DAYS

Most nights we would lie in our beds, my brother and I, listening to the radio music, allowing it to melt us into sleep. His Sears clock radio would play fifteen minutes and then click itself off, a snooze button that led straight into sleep. Disk jockeys always mellowed out after 10 o'clock, giving us the comfort of the Sky Liners or the love ballads of Connie Francis and Paul Anka. It was snooze music alright played against the distant rumble or the mills, the steady climb of truck transmissions on the highway outside. It was headlights moving across the wall; it was our breathing soft and deep into the distance of night.

*   *   *

Mother kept the radio going in the kitchen all the time. Local news or call-in talk filled the room of her loneliness, her girl voice singing the band music as she ironed. Once I watched her and my father dancing across the linoleum. But mostly it was her singing alone.

That day I stood eating her box cake at the counter. Her soft voice at the sink telling my brother and me that she had miscarried. We setting down our cake as our father rose to hold her again in his arms, and no radio on.

*   *   *

Driving the car, all we had was AM, but we knew the dial, the chrome push buttons taking us quick from Steubenville to Weirton to Pittsburgh, from rock to standards to rhythm and blues. It would sing away the miles, become more real than the road, the mills, the hills and abandoned barns, radio taking us where we wanted to go.

*   *   *

Sitting together that first time in my brother's car on the ridge, we would look out through trees above the valley. I would take her hand and kiss her fingers, gently moving her closer. The windows would be down, bird song in the dusk, and softly Johnny Mathis would croon "Chances Are," her hair smelling of night flowers, her skin warm to touch. As I felt her breathing close beside me, the Everly

Brothers would be pleading, "Let It Be Me." Each song had our names on it: "This I Swear," "Baby, I'm Yours" – that melting touch, that truth singing through our hearts.

TRACK MEET

We dress lightly in the thin running gear of shorts and shirts, slide the school's soft sweatsuits over our bare legs and arms, track shoes hugging our feet. Our casual talk of school and girls echoes off locker room walls. We take a last sip of water at the fountain, go through the smell of lineament and soap, out into the warm Spring night, twilight fading slowly into the electric glow of stadium lights.

We kick into a lap around the track, loosening up, getting focused, breezing past the high jump pit, the long jump track, the dark football scoreboard, around the goal post of the 200, in along the huge cement block of the stadium bleachers where girls and parents gather. Suddenly we dash past them and the two lanes of warm-up hurdles and starting blocks tossed along the grass.

It feels good, all of it. Thoughts of competition lie buried in the gut. I stand at the end breathing hard the night air and look out across the stadium fence into the dark shadows of the steel mills, hear the warning hoot of trains along the river, smell an odor of smoke, a fragrance of cut grass.

On the hill behind me the town nestles in tiers of houses with their porch lights on and rising to a crest among the woods. We are far from the traffic of town, out in the mill flats along the creek.

Ours is another kind of work. Here we run and leap, toss the shot put for all we are worth, with all that we have to give to the team. Each of us doing his own, besting himself, each event flowing into the next, an effort collective, brothers handing the baton.

UNCLE RAY

We were cruising in his Mercury, the women left behind–
Uncle Ray's stories and laughter, his leaving the radio loud. Ray
would drive us down Route 7 past Ohio River towns: Bridgeport–
Shadyside– Powhattan Point–New Martinsville–Marietta–over the
river at Ravenwood into the heart of his West Virginia. All of us
breathed the smoke of his Chesterfield's as we headed down toward
Charleston, south of the Kanawha River, to his home of Cocoa, West
Virginia, not on any map I've ever seen. It was nestled among the lush
green hills that rose around us as we snaked along roads lined with
trees, over mining creeks, winding like a rope to his folks' front yard.

Soon we would be standing near the hill corn whose silk we
would smoke with cousin Charles Ray. Small and quick, he guided us,
took us out along the creek, taught us to make a pipe from an acorn
and a hollow stick, shared his girly magazines with us behind the barn,
and filled our heads with tales of sex till we too were lusting after
cows.

Uncle Ray would become boy-like around his chubby Ma, his
tobacco spitting Pa. His brothers would tease him into an easy grin. We
boys were fed and loved our fill.

*　　　*　　　*

My brother taught me at seven how to talk Sharon into going
into Grandma's chicken coop. Then how to get her to strip among the
rakes and shovels, let me touch her berry breasts among the smell of
chickens and straw. He was ready to move on, so I was given Sharon,
but she too had learned from him and soon had me standing naked
beside her in the broken window light. Mostly we stood and watched
each other; sometimes we pressed our lips together leaning against the
chicken wire.

Once Uncle Ray opened the door on us standing in bare
sunlight, then shut it quick and never spoke a word.

*　　　*　　　*

Ray drove truck for Penn-Ohio, parked his cab out front most
nights. He liked to drink and stay out late, but he never hurt anyone that

we could see. Once he borrowed Dad's good set of socket wrenches, then left them somewhere and replaced them with a set "bought at the damn five and dime," I can still hear my father telling my mother. Ray loved his baby son, and danced with my Aunt Bay. You couldn't stay mad at Ray for long, even when my brother told me Ray had a girlfriend up river.

*   *   *

Ray worked hard but tired easily. He was always ready for a cigarette break. He smoked two packs a day and used to cough for twenty minutes each morning. Then one Sunday while in church, we were called out and told, "Your uncle Ray has died."

UNCLE HARRY

I remember my bachelor uncle pulling into their driveway in his new DeSoto, his lunch pail banging at his knees as he rushed inside the house of my grandmother. It was a "stroke" they said, and though she recovered, she never spoke again to anyone. Not too unlike my uncle who had to be pried for anything save talk of baseball. He cared for her day and night in that blue twilight of her forgetting.

Mother told us once of Uncle's coming home from war to marry a girl he'd written to, how he bought his wedding shoes but never wore them, put them away in a box. Something closed off then that he never dared tp open again, yet we knew of his longing for women and how he must have dreamed of meeting and caring for that perfect one.

Each month his *Esquire* magazine would arrive wrapped in brown paper, on which he scored the ballgames over radio. My brother and I would sneak them out of his bedroom desk and allow our eyes to touch the Vargas drawings of women perfect in their voluptuousness. And when Uncle left the mill each year for his vacations, he would visit the girly shows in Cleveland and Paris. We'd find the programs and pictures that told of another life. When his sister would introduce him to her women friends, he would slip upstairs by himself and read.

He had no friends that we ever met, yet he loved his garden, his cars, our dad—his brother, his mother and sister, the Cleveland Indians, and us boys he would take on trips to New England, the Grand Canyon, Yellowstone, the Everglades.

When he died, we sang "Take Me out to the Ballgame." around his grave. His money helped build this back porch where we sit now in sun and shade.

WAYS OF MOVING

Just walking through my town. It became a way of thinking, stepping through memories like tree shadows across the street and into the new light of thoughts, walking free and steady in the street. I could be coming home from school, climbing the hill to the neighborhood store, strolling home at night from my girlfriend's house, my face still flush with springtime kissing—walking from and to and all the in-between. Walking through and into myself, being inside the change, each step a breath, a threshold, a soft sure echoing.

*　　*　　*

Delivering papers in the early morning, as the birds awoke, I'd toss the papers softly onto the porches, sticking some beneath mail boxes, dropping others inside storm doors. I would roll them as I walked, folding and turning them back into logs for tossing.

The Wheeling *Intelligencer* and the Pittsburgh *Post Gazette*—each to each, and mine to keep them straight, get them there before folks went off to work. My own father waking as I returned, climbing my way back inside the covers, my school clothes already on, my face still wanting to be washed, my hair combed straight and back on my head.

It was Father then who woke me with the words, "It's time, son. Time to wake up." Then he padded down the stairs and out the door to work.

We both were doing commerce, making our way.

*　　*　　*

On Sundays we would go for "a family drive," strolling the countryside for hours in our Plymouth, ending at a pottery shop where we kids would run among the bird baths and ceramic elves. Mother would browse inside finding a butter plate, a candy dish, or an ashtray shaped like a flat tire. It was endless the way she could look, touching everything with her soft hands as she walked.

And we would stand around the pop machine begging with our eyes, sending our sister to ask it. And when there were coins in his pockets we would all sip the sweet soda of a cold Ne-Hi Orange or Dad's Rootbeer.

Heading home along the river, Father would begin to sing, "On Top of Old Smokey," "Down By the Old Mill Stream,"and "Up a Lazy River." Eventually the only way to stand it would be to join in. All of us singing full-voiced against the approaching dusk.

*   *   *

This motion we live in, not to lose nor to win; the motion off a swing, letting go with the hands, lifting off the seat, and gliding, gliding through moments into the wide and open air.

BROTHERS

The high school teachers called me my brother's name, though we didn't look the same. And I followed his shoe prints a long time, stepping carefully, but then where he went long, I went short; where he did numbers, I did words. And yet we both played it safe, sat in the same row at church, came home the same pathway through the yard. You see, it was never an insult to be compared to him, though it could become a pain.

*　　　*　　　*

Once a girl invited me to a dance because he had turned her down, something that dawned on me like a toothache as we stood near the bleachers watching him and his date. Darlene was nice though, let me dance close and bought us Isaley's sundaes afterwards, but I couldn't finish mine and didn't walk her home. That night in our beds, after the lights went off, he whispered calmly, "I could have told you, if you'd asked."

*　　　*　　　*

He was always running ahead of me. In Boy Scouts, I'd be Tenderfoot to his Star, Star to his Life. Thank god, neither of us made it all the way to Eagle. Those merit badges became too heavy, started to smell like work—"Housekeeping," for Pete's sake. And "Bicycling" nearly killed us both as we wound along the traffic of Route Seven for 20 miles.

A decade later I was recalling getting lost following map directions and my scout master father said, "Yeah? I don't remember that. Was that the same night your brother found the treasure?" It was words like that that made me find my own friends and create my own trouble.

David had made a high jumping pit in our back yard. I jumped the stadium fence with Freddy Bickerstaff. He won my father's praise and a load of sawdust. I got busted by the city police for trespassing. It went like that for a while, him going straight, me going wide, but when spring track meets started, we would run the mile relay together,

I the second leg and he the third, and until he graduated, I was always an inch below his high jump mark.

*   *   *

We never really dated the same girl, though we both were sweet on Joyce. She grew up with us, taught us to talk and dance with girls. You could hold her closer than a sister, and at birthday parties, she would still choose you at kissing games. We laughed at each other's jokes. We all exchanged Christmas gifts.

The only times David and I double dated were for a Christmas formal or a prom where he would drive the old Chevy wagon, and my date and I would climb onto the sheet-covered backseat. We'd split up at the dance, though I'd watch him joking with his friends. Later he'd drop me and my date off at her place, and I'd wonder in the mess of bra snaps and crinolines if he were still as good at reading maps and finding buried treasure.

*   *   *

I was his best man, and he was mine. We married friends, and live in different towns.

INSIDE THE NOISE

Yes, there were coal mines, and steel mills, and factories. All of them grinding away at the edge of things—thin shudder of the earth that we lived with, echoing roar of river inside the hills.

It grew inside us.

It was the sound of a furnace under the floor shaking the boards at our feet. Men and women who worked long in it dissolved to deafness, began to speak with hands. Those who lived along its edge learned to turn away.

Birds stood on fence posts, without any necks, or flitted close to the ground.

Open any window, close any door, it was there, a slow and steady rain that fell over everything. It was a death rattle there in our chest, and our lives were clothes hanging out on the line without rest.

Everyone knew but no one spoke.

ALONG THE EDGE OF THINGS
A LIGHT IS FOUND: DREAMWORK

Dressing for work I see two dogs fighting across the street. I watch them clearly from the bedroom window. The large one is slow and sick, and the small one keeps biting at his behind. I cannot hear them, and I close my eyes.

*   *   *

I walk through town, oblivious to sound. At the baker's window I see a customer undress before the counter, a row of cup cakes inside. At the newsstand old women are loading toy wagons pulled by dogs. They do their work without talk. The dogs' mouths are muzzled with rags. The barber's candy cane sign is not turning, yet the shop is full of children spinning in the chairs while their parents clap. An old man dressed as a woman walks beside me. His face is down till we reach the corner. A mustache rides his ruby lip. He looks down again and we spit together, waiting for the light.

*   *   *

I am standing on the street waiting for a bus. A woman with long red hair and yellow dress gets on. Her arms are full and when she takes her daughter's hand, her skirt blows up like music. She turns to see me watch, smiles as I lean further into brick, a flock of pigeons at my feet.

*   *   *

I come into an empty house. All is still, the quiet of nails in a box. I walk through the dark to the kitchen where the stove's gas flames are alive with light. I stand in water to my ankles. The furnace comes on. The stairs creak. An envelope is found.

ALONG THE EDGE

Over the fence at the top of the hill, we slide down the dark gravel onto the tracks where for a moment we pause, listen, then dash over rails and thick ties in a boy's death dance. Hearts pounding in our chests, we look back, then vanish into thickets at the other side.

A path dumps us out onto old Route 7 where we walk along the roadside kicking up dust and waving our fishing poles to the few cars whizzing by. Then in a moment we are gone, down the bank beside the bridge at Cross Creek.

Under its shadows and heavy beams the soft roar of cars passes overhead. Along the stream bank we file, our poles pointing ahead to river and sky. In my backpack, our line and hooks already tangled, our worms and doughball wrapped in foil; in my brother's, our sandwiches and drinks.

Near the stadium fence the caretaker rides high on his mower, giving us a wave as we walk under the railroad bridge. A flock of crows in the thick bushes, a nest of robins in the Locust tree. We cross mill tracks past slag heaps, yell back above the roar of engines and blast furnace. At the river s edge our green creek turns river brown, and we stare out at the wide waters, then weave our way down to our spots.

Seated on fallen branches and abandoned railroad tie, we dig our boots into thick tufted grass knowing even then how weeds hold the banks. Beside the rushing waters we bait up, cast out our thin lines, and wait. The sun bakes our minds, a coal barge glides down river, a hawk floats overhead, and we trade stories and jokes.

At the noon whistle we eat bologna sandwiches and chips. Ken spills water from the canteen onto Hatcher's head. An old man, at the point, takes a leak into the river. All afternoon we catch fish and tangle lines. The catfish take the hook, shoot out of the water thick and whiskered, ready to pay you back as you tear the hook from their lips; the bass you have to play along, listen for the strike and hook them up and away; heavy bodied carp you curse proudly and throw back.

In the first measure of dusk we carry our haul on the path back home, along the thin edge of our fathers' work.

AT SIXTEEN

I waited to get my licence till I was almost seventeen, a month after my mother got hers at thirty-six.

That same month I took the car to drive Kenny home, past the playground where the older guys were playing full court. I was smiling over at a group of girls in their summer shorts when the car drifted into a telephone pole. Everyone stopped except Kenny who smacked his head against the window. They all watched as I shifted into reverse, then sped up the hill.

At Kenny's house his bump had grown to egg size. He had stopped cursing long enough to check out the car with me—the bent bumper and the broken teeth of the grill, my brother's '57 Chevy. We stared, sighed, then laughed out loud in the street. I sweated it all the way home.

I had no licence, and so Mom took the rap for the insurance company.

"You owe me one," she said, as I ran the sweeper along the couch.

*   *   *

That summer I sold bottles of Ne-Hi pop in front of the Kroger's, the Top Value stamps sticking to my fingers as I made change in the hot sun. My girlfriend's mother got me the job, and it paid a dollar an hour.

During those two weeks, at night I'd sit with Barbara alone on the couch, kissing her soft cheeks and lips, eating her mother's sweet rolls loaded with butter.

*   *   *

As a sophomore I played basketball, rode the bench on the reserve team waiting for the older guys to pass on to varsity. I'd sit and stare into the crowd watching the faces, joking with my friends. Then one night in Follansbee, I watched the pace of the game like it was a movie. I locked into it. We were playing tired without any rhythm, down ten points with all the empty energy of a sleepy child.

When the coach sent me in to spell off a starter, I came alive—
making my own pace, razing their guards, grabbing the ball away, fast
breaking it down court til they had to hit me under the bucket. In three
minutes we were only two points down. The coach motioned Time
Out, and the crowd roared. Everyone likes a good fight. A couple
guys started patting my ass, "Way to go in there." My buddies cheered
from the bench, throwing me a towel. The coach wrapped his arm
round my shoulder, said, "I don't know what you've been eating, but
I'm ordering it for all you guys."

I started the next two games till I began hearing the crowd, fell
in love with the praise, shooting too much and too hard. I drifted back
to my place on the bench, but by then the spring wind was already
calling, sending me running out the road towards track season.

*   *   *

That year I read *The Catcher in the Rye*. My mother put it (and
thereby all literature) into my hands, the copy with a drawing of
Holden in his hunter's cap on the cover. I read it all that night, laughing
my brother awake till I had to sneak down stairs to the couch. I
finished it with a beer.

Salinger had one thing wrong though. I didn't want to call him
up for a Coke. I wanted to ask old Holden to walk with me to school
next day where we'd lean against the brick wall, just laughing our asses
off at all the phoney bastards.

That weekend I wrote my first short story.

RUNNING INTO THE NIGHT

The stadium lights recorded our triumph. The mile relay was always run last and almost always determined the meet. Outside the fence, the deep roar of the blast furnaces and the quick clash of the freight trains marked the events. I and my brother would run legs three and four that night.

I remember sliding off my sweats, folding them onto the bench, then jumping up and down to keep warm in the April air. "Stay up with him," coached my brother, "And if you can get a lead, kick it home." On the side of the track we practiced handing off the baton with Jim and Tom. We drew our lane, then paced around to keep loose. Weeks ago I had pulled a muscle on the final curve and had to be carried in.

Neither of us said anything, but we kept checking the crowd for Dad's red jacket. Our eyes told each other he must have pulled a double or the car had broken down. The coach called us over, "Okay, we're behind again by one point. It's all up to you guys." We read the ground, each other's eyes. "Just run a good race," he called and walked away.

That night we were invincible. Don't ask me why. Each runner stepped out ahead at least a stride, so that I stretched it out to a good yard. Dave took the stick in his hand coming up and kicked it all the way, under four minutes. My lungs were still burning as he passed the flag pole releasing the roar of the crowd. We had brought it home like we never would again.

*　　　*　　　*

When Uncle Ray came into the locker room, we were still in the showers singing "La Bamba." He came over to David who then turned to me. "Dad's in the hospital. His appendix burst." We were dressed and out of there in five minutes. Uncle Ray drove like a maniac up the Steubenville streets to the Ohio Valley Hospital. "Go on in," he called through the dark. "I'll park this thing."

I think it was then I started hating hospitals—their fatal numbness, the sickening antiseptic smell, the hallways all full of dread.

When we first saw Dad I thought he was dead. He lay there so pale and weak with needles and tubes running into his arms like a sick carburetor. Mute and cold I wanted someone's words. *Orphans,* I thought to myself, though it didn't make sense, and then Mom was hugging us. "He's recovering. He was hit hard with it while rushing home to get to your damn track meet." I took a breath, the first it seemed in hours. "My God," she said, "Look at you. You're white as a ghost!" Everyone stared at my naked face so that I could not hide my pain or my sorrow.

When she asked about the track meet, I still couldn't talk. David and I just stood there mute by Dad's bedside until he opened his eyes.

GRADUATING

We were called down to the principal's office, like two
hooligans from Civics class, Mr. Rodak shouting, "Larry and Kenny!"
I turned my gaze from the windows to his bare face and head. "You
two...to the principal's...Now, go!" We walked, my best friend and I,
down the long echoing hallway, past a hundred mute photos of classes
from the past. He whispering, "Hey, what you do?" And I, "Me—
how about you?" We had made it through four years without such
reprimand in a school where most sons and daughters of millwrights
and cashiers, brakemen and nurses aides, left school for jobs in the
mills and factories. Only Kenny and I, Barbara and Peter, Marilyn and
Jim, Guy and Patty were headed for college or nurse's training. We
were the 10 percent who somehow went on, taking less traveled roads
away from all we had ever known, including each other.

At the office door we met the school secretary, Mrs. Quinn.
"Relax, boys," she laughed. "It's good news. Go on in." Inside was
Shirley, her fair face smiling up at us, her clear blue eyes the same we
had known since first grade. Early on we had walked together to
school for years, holding hands as we crossed the streets. By fifth
grade we all knew she was smarter than any of us and poorer in a town
where poor was the norm. Freshman year Shirley chose the business
track.

"What's up?" I asked, and she, "I think they've chosen our
valedictorian." In the glare of the office window, we read each other's
faces, the mill roaring softly outside. And so we sat there knowing we
had made it, the three of us sharing the honors of a small steeltown.
And yet we had only competed with ourselves. Our gym buddies and
prom dates had long ago withdrawn from the game.

Mr. Muth entered the room and took my hand first, as he had
at track meets. "Congratulations, Larry, you're first. We're all proud,

as we know your folks will be." I turned to my friends, their soft clear eyes, "You two tied for second," he said, adding, "I have to tell you, there was only a decimal point between you all." A decimal point— we grinned at that, knowing how our junior year Shirley had gone to work at the A&P after school to help out her mom, while Kenny and I ran the clubs, played basketball, ran track under the lights and racked up points. Everyone knew it was unfair, yet no one spoke of it. Finally we friends just smiled and shook each other's hands like the adults we would become: Kenny to military college and engineering in D.C., me following my brother into liberal arts and a teaching career, Shirley to cashier work at the local bank, then bank manager in Wheeling, all of us married now.

And so I gave the commencement speech that night in 1961 to the crowded auditorium, quoting Kennedy's "Ask not what your country can do for you, but what you can do for your country." Only that night for all of us gathered there, "our country" still meant our town, our families, and our friends.

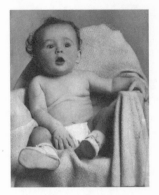

Infant Larry, 1943

David and Larry, 1945

Parents Deb and Jean with
Larry and David, 1945

Deb with boys on Murdock Street

Smith Brothers in southern Ohio, Murray, Mont, Ernest
(grandfather), Wilmer, and Bundy, c. 1930's

Harry, Carrie, and Ernest Smith,
1945, year of Ernest's death

Mother and Grandmother Putnam
father and grandfather Raymond
Putnam with boys, 1946

Cowboy Larry, 1950

Polio shots given by Drs. Riney & Albaugh,
Mingo Central Elementary School, c. 1955

Janis, Larry, & David, 1951   Larry & Debbie, Murdock Street 1957

View of Wheeling-Pitt Steel Mill from Mingo school windows

Larry in high school, 1959   310 Murdock Street, Mingo Junction, Ohio
Family home 1955-1985

Graduating Class of 1961, *Note Larry, Kenny, Barbara, Shirley

Graduation photo of Larry, 1961
Classmates outside Mingo Central High

Part Two

(Photo © James Jeffrey Higgins)

I know what we call it
Most of the time.
But I have my own song for it,
And sometimes, even today,
I call it beauty

-James Wright, "Beautiful Ohio"

STARTING COLLEGE

My folks dropped me off at college that first time, driving the three hours across middle Ohio to New Concord, where astronaut John Glenn grew up near the fields and hills that held Muskingum College. With his wife Annie, he went there, where the students almost outnumbered the locals. Muskingum College—a small Christian college for small Christians, that's what the upperclassman joked during Frosh Week. I had won the valedictorian scholarship of $400, and so followed my brother out of town off into the land of college—*1961*.

* * *

Everything seemed so Presbyterian there—the red brick buildings spaced neatly around the quad, the dorms for girls and guys kept on separate hills, the twice weekly chapels of lectures and prayers where girls in plaid jumpers checked our attendance and guys in white bucks and button-down minds strutted and grinned. The professors joked or scowled while filling our minds with numbers and words, new ideas that were really old. I loved and hated it, taking me so far from home. Everyone seemed so neurotically smart there, especially my roommate whom I watched at our window the next day capturing flies. He would pin them to his bulletin board where he pulled off their wings, cremating some with lighter fluid and a match. *Everything.*

* * *

That first day my folks stood in my dorm room looking around at the desks, the closet, the bed; the closet, the desks, the bed. Mom, helping me make the bed right for the last time that semester. Dad, not knowing where to sit, standing in the doorway trying to smile, thinking, *So this is college.* Finally, my saying "Hey, let's go get us a cup of coffee," and we drove out to the diner on Main Street for a piece of pie. None of us knowing what to say. Finally them pulling away because I insisted I wanted to walk back across campus to my dorm, when all I really wanted was to jump into that driver's seat and gas it all the way home.

When I got back to my room that night, I wrote two letters. One to my girlfriend back home and one to my folks thanking them for all they had given me.

HITCHING A RIDE

I would write those college letters home to Barbara, lifelines really to a world I had abandoned to survive. The letters were going out faster than they arrived. I didn't care. I needed to write them, to hear myself as I knew I was then and there.

*   *   *

On weekends I would pack my bag and head down the long hill, past trees and pond, the college chapel onto Main Street, New Concord. Route 40 traffic would be as sparse as beers in this Christian town. I would walk east to the edge of town, set my bag down on the berm, my sign stuck to its side, "Ride to Steubenville," close enough. The autumn wind pushing leaves along would blow at my face. Eventually a trucker or salesman would pull off the road ahead, and I would run toward the window, his hand motioning me in.

*   *   *

I would enter our house without knocking, hear them calling, "Look who's home!" And Mother would fix me a plate from supper that I would eat sitting on the couch with them before the television, waiting for them to ask...anything. We would talk of my ride, how the school was feeding me, when I'd need to head back. My sisters would sit near me, and I would smile into their shining faces—a brother again.

*   *   *

Next morning I would drive up to Barbara's house, kiss the music of her face in the doorway. And we would drive out to Jefferson Lake, park in the woods by the lake. My fingers would trace the map of her skin, the October sun of her warm breasts pressing inside me, the sweetness of her mouth opening. We spoke silence, touching the membrane of our love. Moment into moment we breathed it, then lay back till the words would come.

*   *   *

My books always lay at the bottom of my bag, and I would not open them till Sunday came. After church and dinner, we would head west, and I would begin again to read my way back into their world.

COLLEGE DAYS

I walk from geology class to the band practice field. We will be marching in the John Glenn Welcome Home Parade. He is a college alumnus and New Concord native, so our campus is invaded by the press and media all week as he circles our earth three times. Trucks and broadcast towers surround the gymnasium where we are to go and watch the event. The second day of this, one of the upperclassmen tells an interviewer, "John Glenn is being sold to the American public like a bar of soap." It gets out and is printed in *Esquire* magazine. He is a campus hero.

The media returns again for the parade, when we all see John and Annie Glenn, riding now on the back of a convertible that we march behind. He waves broadly, she quietly smiles beneath the spring maples, and we are all proud to be a part of their world.

*　　*　　*

That next fall I walk back to my room, a club-dorm, not a fraternity, and I throw my books on my bed and head down to the kitchen where I work scrubbing pans. It is an old house with a friendly cook, Mrs. Shepard, who knows us like a mother and allows us to snack. I am a sophomore studying literature and stuffing my own poems into an already crowded drawer. From notebook to typewriter to drawer, that's their journey for now. I am taking the survey course in American literature, falling in love with each new period ...Romanticist ...Realist ...Naturalist ...Thoreau ...Mark Twain ...Stephen Crane. In the humanities I have found a home, a deep connection to the world of people and places.

I enter the kitchen and join the crew. I am putting on my apron when I hear the booming voice of Paul Shafer, political genius of our club. "This is absurd, you know, eating food and washing dishes on the day before we all die." No one speaks but we each look up. "The news, man, aren't you guys listening to the news! The Russians are going to launch their rockets on us ...The Cuban Crisis, it's about to explode in our faces. We all could be dead by morning." Mel is a nut, but he knows his stuff. "Hey, Mrs. C," he calls, "what's for dinner?"

"Pot roast," she answers, "And you get out of here with that talk." I stare out the one window. We all have this shift to do, this food to serve, these dishes and pots to clean, then study for a tomorrow that may never come. There is this dull movement about things as we do our jobs, and for some reason I think about the albino girl in my lit class, her too fair skin, her delicate eyes, her stillness walking to and from class, this sense of intense fragility hovering over everything.

*　　　*　　　*

It is my junior year, a cold November day in 1963, and I am walking back from my education class. I am passing the class, but the teacher is an old retired school superintendent who goes off all the time...lectures and stories out of the thinning hair of his memory. We have to listen to his prejudices of minorities, his tirades of legislators, his broken record of successes. I hate this guy. Why don't they get rid of him? I have to take this course to become a teacher, yet I am doubting the whole profession.

I walk back to my club-dorm down along the stadium track where the leaves are blown along the fence, and I watch people hurrying back to their dorms moving away from class. It is three o'clock, and there is no mail for me in my box. My girlfriend has not written for weeks. She is too busy with her life, and I feel like those autumn leaves. Then I see all the guys gathered around the television listening for all their life. I hear "Once again, the President has been shot in Dallas, Texas, this afternoon. We are waiting for a medical report..." I sit on the floor. *My God, Kennedy shot. My God, I don't believe it. What kind of monster? What kind of life?* No one knows what to say to this and we all wait in quiet till: "Ladies and Gentlemen, this just in, President John F. Kennedy has been shot and killed in Dallas, Texas, this day." All my problems vanish in the dull pain of knowing this and feeling how it will never ever change. Our President is dead.

The next week I go to Education and Society class, and there is another professor there. He is standing before the desk telling us that Professor Wentworth was taken to the hospital late last night and died early this morning of a heart attack. Class will be dismissed until something can be arranged. It is a November of regret.

*　　*　　*

I am sitting in the college library watching the faces of girls leaning over books—their smoothe hair, clear eyes, the softness of sun through windows. And I—I cannot find a topic for a persuasive speech. I have no ground beneath my feet, and so I drift through afternoon.

Others come and go. I lean back to stay awake, turn to look away from her dark eyes. Here are rows of slim books—*Topics for National Debate*. I take one down, and it opens to "Japanese Americans: The Internment Camps." I read long of those days when Americans could not tell our Japanese brothers from those who had bombed Pearl Harbor. I hear how they were taken from their homes and land, locked inside U.S. concentration camps, how they were forced to make a life somewhere else. I hold the book close and steady, begin taking notes. I know this book is reference, but I smuggle it out at dusk, as I would a brother. Their song of injustice joins my own, and on Monday morning, I rise to sing the voice collective.

*　　*　　*

And two things more. In the spring of 1962 a young guy publishes a story in the school's literary magazine, *The Angry I*. It is about two lovers making it in a hayloft. Everyone reads it, and then the magazine is shut down, the student is expelled. There is a whispered outrage; he is our fallen martyr of truth and art. Finally a couple faculty members rise to insist on his rights. He is reinstated and will graduate though his name 'David Budbill' is announced through clenched teeth.

The following spring I am walking from class along the track road when I spot a 45 record in its sleeve lying beneath the trees. I pick it up. Its bright orange label reads, *From Me to You—The Beatles*. I take it back to my little room and play it over and over. It is a new season, a time of change.

ENDING IT

I wake to the sound of mourning doves in the front yard under mill clouds raining down on us their constant weather, a storm echoing inside. And I lie on the mattress remembering her eyes that cut deeper than words, severing her life from mine. The roar of blast furnace echoes it inside this hollow room where the old ceiling maps my pain.

*　　*　　*

His footsteps on the stairs, my father going out the door where she had stood handing me back the ring, so light and hard yet breaking everything. The train calling out as it ran over us again and again.

*　　*　　*

It is a season of dogs barking in the high grass, her voice already gone, a dry, hard wind crying through the yard.

REMEMBERING JOYCE

> ". . . The closer you get
> to things, the more you see, the less you understand."
> -Philip Levine

I held you close that night on the dance floor, the music turning us around in the little club in Weirton, where we had sipped our rum and cokes while Kenny drank too much Vodka. We had driven out to this place you knew above the mill flats where no one knew us and the band was live, playing Buddy Holly songs. Kenny and I were home from our colleges, friends become like distant cousins. We could no longer find the looks and words to share. He soon found a dark haired woman to buy drinks for leaning at the bar. And you, dressed in tight black skirt and sweater, were left to hear me moan about my broken heart after four years of almost loving her. I drank again and grew quiet. Your brown eyes were so lovely even there in the darkness: my oldest friend, born to mothers who laughed together on front porches, fathers who fished together. All through school I'd watched you as a sister turn from chubby girl to beautiful young woman charming the guys yet going steady with no one. In band I marched behind your majorette legs, lifting the trumpet to my lips to sing.

*   *   *

But this night I'm remembering was another thing. Your answering my call, breaking a Saturday date, to take us guys with you to dance again. It was you, of course, who had taught me to dance in our living room, as the 45's fell lightly, spinning us into jitterbug and twists, shaking the lampshades with our laughter. And it was you too who taught my feet to move my legs, slow dancing to love songs.

And that was how it happened that night as the music turned from rock to the slowest, sad ballad ever sung. Ritchie Valens' "Donna" pulled us closer than we'd ever been. I held you in the darkness more than friends as those tragic lyrics of poor dead Ritchie kept crooning "Oh, Donna" breaking my heart again and again till I closed my eyes holding you and crossed some crazy line to where you were her again in my arms and not the real Joy of my life. You felt it right away yet waited out the song to pull back, move away, leaving me in the shadows of what might have been for her, for us.

*   *   *

How Kenny got home that night, I'm not sure. It was near the end with him. What I do remember, besides your arms and soft breathing next to me in the little car, is saying goodbye to you under the streetlight, each of us knowing somehow something had been broken.

TEACH ME TONIGHT

for Ann

My heart was broken when we met, a loss that wanted to teach me something I couldn't grasp till I met you. You helped me to love deeply, to value your silences, your language of touch and looks, your being part of a family like mine who cared about things. In your eyes I read the movement of flowers, the shadow-flight of birds.

*   *   *

We were from the same hometown, grown up blocks apart—you in your Catholic Italian tribe, me in my Irish-German clan. We knew each other without words. I played my guitar out the bedroom window loud enough for you to hear on your grandmother's back porch. You would walk around the corner in your Catholic cheerleader's uniform, the blue-pleated skirt, your white bobby sox. We lived near enough to watch, beside our town's big river.

*   *   *

On our first date that summer your mother met me at the door. I had gone to your grandmother's house, and you had moved. Your mother rode up the hill with me in my uncle's car. She told me they had gone to school together. She knew my family well. The car took the hills, shifting down to climb. You came to the door surprised to see us together, what would become of these two streams of your life. You were wearing a navy blue dress with a white trim and were lovely pouring me a soda. I thanked the sun and stars for bringing us together in that little room. We sat on the couch to talk. Outside I could barely hear the whiz of traffic, the roar of the mills, the clash of trains. It was a curtain of sound we both lived inside.

*   *   *

At the movie you cried at the best parts, touched my arm to let me know you were entering my life. It was the first week of June 1964, and we were watching *The Carpetbaggers* at the Paramount Theatre in downtown Steubenville. On the drive home I spoke of how the man in the film didn't know how to love, and you listened and smiled. The movie ran long, so I took you straight home. We stood outside the door a long time making plans. When you laughed, I took your hand. We kissed in the moonlight and your teaching me began.

BECOMING PART OF IT

And when we met our love in each other, we held it close sitting in the car feeling the moments pass.

I had found with you a family—your quiet Hungarian father, your strong Italian mother, your happy younger sister hugging you till I grew jealous–and they all lived together in their fine brick house, while you were off becoming a nurse down river in Wheeling.

And there was more—your grandmother two blocks away where we would walk to have tea around the table and listen to her tales of coming here, twice from Italy—the young girl she was when Pop arranged to marry her and the children they had together—nine who lived in that little house along the railroad.

Other times there were crowds of aunts and uncles taking turns at the spaghetti and bread, the cellar wine, each one stealing the floor to tell a story, sing a song, dance the tarantella or the jitterbug.

And I who sat along the wall beside the heater watched this musical, this feature film, played out in kitchen light—so many strong character actors—I prayed it would never end.

But then it did as I saw too the comic-sad opera of anguish and love passed round like wedding soup, how spite sometimes spoiled the sauce: nine children raised by an ailing mother and her eldest daughter, your mother, a child raising children who couldn't get enough love to eat, though Mom and Pop kept the house warm, food on the table, tomatoes and peppers in the garden.

It was a novel I read but could not understand.

And you and I would sit out on the back porch near the grape arbor eating figs and hearing the voices inside, the crickets in the bushes, our hands pressing together the new rhythm of our lives.

SUNLIGHT WALKING

And we walk out from town, over the hill, past the houses along the road to the woods where we both stand fresh in the trees and kissing the sunlight on lips tender as turning leaves. Wood thrush enter our hearts, and your eyes begin to sing as we hold together there, our skin lighting each breath our first and last as I press through you.

   *   *   *

And in my pocket I feel the key I've brought with me, the worn key to the house on the road, the one my father is soon to tear down for lumber, making a way for the road to come. I haven't told you of this key grown warm in my hand, as we sat now inside the silence of the fallen tree.

   *   *   *

Your hand. Your soft arms. Your face clear and warm near me. Your tongue across my lips. I want to carry you there to the house and the window where we can lie in the sunlight of our clothes, enter you more deeply than stream flows into river. There will be time enough for everything.

   *   *   *

A car passes, its tires speaking to the road and I think of time again as the sunlight fades, then returns. We are dreaming into each other here in this woods beside the road, our words turned into branches and grass, thin echo of sparrows. There are voices far away, some we have always known counting backwards to before we were born. We listen and know we will return to them along the road we came.

   *   *   *

Some other day we will walk out and enter the small house for which we have made this threshold.

BAPTISM BY FIRE AND WATER

That summer I entered the world of the mills where my father labored forty years.

I am told to walk down through the sparks shooting out of the hot ladles of slag. *Go on*, they say, *You can walk right through.*

The alley between building and wall is darkness but for the hot glow of steel and slag. Clouds from the blast furnace block the sun, and fear grips down in me. *My first day*, I think, *and I will perish in flames and smoke.*

Go on, they say again, *They're expecting you.*

And so I step into it, down the tracks along walls of the dark burned brick. What prayers I know are said blind and quick.

*   *   *

At the alley's end a stairway and a huge man at the top waves me on. I cannot hear my own boots on the metal steps, just the roar of furnace and trains, more than any ocean. Before me men in robes of asbestos—shining silver, masked in helmets and goggles—face the heat, dance a ritual in the golden glow.

And I think, *If I step wrongly here, one foot will turn to slag, the other to steel. I am too young*, grips my throat while the liquid light melts me, breaks me before its truth.

Suddenly someone is pulling my arm and I step back through a door quickly shut, into a room full of men sweating in shirt sleeves. Red faces smudged with ore read my own.

Here, put this on. We need you up front. You're the relief, someone shouts, and they all laugh. As I dress in asbestos, someone hands me his gloves, *You'll need these*, and I realize that I too am laughing. As we walk into the heat, we are all ready to die, my fear fallen at my feet into the rough trough of liquid fire.

WEDDING BELLS, BLUE AND WHITE

We were wed in innocence one July day in 1965. The sun was high as we walked down the aisle. The reception was close and filled with people we loved. And we, we were the plastic bride and groom atop the wedding cake, watching and smiling as the marriage rites unfolded around us.

*   *   *

From college and nurse's school, we had come home to a place where we no longer belonged, and so we searched out and found a summer apartment above a piano teacher in Steubenville. Ann began work at the hospital, I in the mills. Our wedding plans had been small: our choice of wedding party and gowns, my choice not to have a mass (a wound still). And so it all unfolded like the red carpet before Ann's steps to the altar.

*   *   *

My brother stood watching me pace in the altar boys' room, our stomach's empty, heads hurting still. His showing me the exit door to the back alley just as the music called us forth. Standing there before them all, Presbyterian boys accompliced to the Catholic priests, watching my bride veiled and lovely come slowly towards me. Her father walked in tears holding tight the whole way. I felt I might have to wrestle her away, but then he gave up her and we stood together at last our hands touching, bleeding into one. All of it softly unfolding: the words, the gestures, the candles, the kiss, the applause and long walk, the shower of rice.

*   *   *

At the family luncheon in the church cafeteria, my parents ushered in guests—my father glad-handing everyone, my mother's laughter chiming a blessing, the warble of words as Ann's mom raced back and forth between the kitchen and the hall, serving us all her wedding soup, her rich pasta and meatballs, the warm rolls and afternoon wine. And we sat watching, my bride and I, eating, nodding, kissing each time to the ringing of glasses tapped for our love.

Bridesmaids and groomsmen flirted, then drove off somewhere for afternoon drinks.

*   *   *

We were dropped off at the house of Ann's parents where we were to wait for five hours till the night reception. And so we sat on her mother's couch across from the window—the plastic bride and groom sitting. *But isn't she mine now? What was all the ceremony for?* I asked no one. Only she knew my heart and whispered with her eyes: "Not yet... Be patient...I love you." Finally I felt myself rise, heard myself saying, "I'm going to go down home. I'll be back in a couple of hours. I love you." My brother walked with me through the crowded kitchen out to our little Fiat. I needed to walk but climbed in, and we drove down the hill. At my parents' house we talked until I stole off upstairs, and slept a last time in my own bed, all covered with clothes.

*   *   *

Back at her house later, we kissed in the kitchen, and as Ann got into the car, I wanted to grab the wheel, drive off with my princess to our own place. But we had none; it would not be ready until we returned from our honeymoon. And so we rode again through the town past grocery stores and bars, blowing the horn and waving, feeling the breeze on our cheeks, laughing.

*   *   *

St. Bernadette's Hall had no air conditioning and so the drinks flowed—high balls and beer, more wine, and soda pop...Ham sandwiches and potato salad, celery sticks and dip. It was who we were then and now, and we greeted everyone, uncles and aunts, cousins and neighbors, until piano music called us onto the dance floor. We moved as one and I did not want to ever let go of her, even to sit down. But of course we did: cutting cake, throwing bouquets and garters, watching our families talk and dance together. Our grandmothers telling each other stories of old houses in their neighborhood. It was all the right clothes to wear but too hot and too long, and so jackets came off, shirt sleeves were rolled, high heels left under tables, windows opened wider to the night air.

*   *   *

Oh, but I wanted her eyes alone. So when the men paid to dance with her, I sat to the side by an old man waiting, drinking a shot and beer, thinking how our Niagara honeymoon would be over in three days. Her mother went around telling men to get up and dance with her, my bride. I knew then that my wrestling for Ann would be with this woman who loved her so. And then the old guy nudged me, and gave me the words, "Take her, son—she's yours"—the day's best blessing. And so we danced in circles, then off the floor to our little car, dragging the cans and signs up to my parents' house, where I threw them into the yard while Ann dressed in a sweet green trousseau suit she had picked for just this time. I shifted gears and we drove north over the hills, past Tappan Lake, towards our honeymoon motel where we kissed and loved, and first showered together. The plastic bride and groom had come off the cake and would not return to our family or our jobs till we were husband and wife.

*   *   *

When my son was four, he stood a long time at the buffet looking up at our wedding photograph, the two of us holding a smile at the altar, and then he spoke, "Mommy, you look so nice. But who is that barber standing beside you?"

TEACHING AND LEARNING

In 1965 I began teaching at Euclid High School outside of Cleveland in one of the best English departments in the state. 3000 students in 3 grades. I had graduated from high school in a class of 65, from Muskingum College in a class of 300. But I was not overwhelmed. I was in my dream career, and Ann was beginning her nursing. Our parents never talked about careers; it was always jobs, "Where you working? What shift? Bummer." I would last three years teaching the willing and the reckless, the challenging and the bored. Bummer.

There were 10 periods and no bells, so it gave the impression of mutual cooperation. Students could have an early or late schedule. Teachers had no choice. We signed in and out, a polite way of punching a time-card. Keeping track of things was worse. My life has been planned hour by hour ever since: grading old papers, recording them and following up, teaching six periods, and always getting ready for tomorrow. Only in moments of perseverance could one burst through the paper trappings to live the moment, speak with care and understanding of what matters, connect with material and readers. But those moments made it all worthwhile.

I became a redeemer of the neglected, a nurturer of the inspired, a guardian of the delinquent. Three sections of general level sophomores, three of college bound juniors. I spoke of American literature as an old college friend. My bulletin board boasted, "Literature Is Life," with photos of common people and titles like *The Grapes of Wrath, The Heart Is a Lonely Hunter.* Those first years I taught in a team, the four of us plotting it out, working in small and large groups, and so I learned from the mistakes and hard-won learnings of others.

It all would have gone fine, were it not for the demands to police and patrol, to monitor hallways and cafeterias and restrooms. I knew I had begun to lose it when I chased a young boy down the hallway, up the stairs, and into his classroom, yelling "You listen to me! Get that shirt-tail tucked in, or you're out of here!" It was the rule that year, and I had swallowed it whole. Another law was that girls had to have skirts that reached the floor when they kneeled. Can you see them kneeling before the principal? Who wouldn't revolt?

But I found myself on the other side. Students saw me as neither their friend nor mentor. They had learned by then to distrust all teachers, except those who allowed them to squander their hopes. "Freedom's just another word for nothing left to lose."

On another front, I was a Kennedy husband and father, valued doubly for teaching in an urban school. I told myself that I would have declared conscientious objector had I been called, but I never had the test. Instead we watched the news of the dying after our meals and listened for our infant daughter nearby in her basinet. As the war mounted, I felt disdain and guilt, no way to make any of it right. And yet our convictions grew their own roots and flowers. It was the worst/best of times.

In 10th period study hall I was hit by enemy fire. I had been coached into prodding the sleepers... "Heads up! Sit up and open a book. No sleeping in this study hall!" when all I wanted to do was take a nap myself, or go out into the still open air of the day. Instead I monitored the aisles. And then I felt it, a "thump" at my back. I looked around. All eyes were down. I bent over and saw fallen on the floor a huge wad of gum. No one person could have made all that. It was an act collective, and it had met its target—the person I watched harassing the others with senseless discipline. I had made myself that target. I was doing what I didn't want to do and being hated for it.

I stood at the back of the room a few minutes catching my breath, then strolled out of the building early that day. I left the school and career that summer. I would find another way of making a living, another way of giving back. We both agreed, we would move south and start graduate school. We would do what it took to survive sane. In 1968 I became a teaching fellow at Kent State University.

HOME BATTLEGROUNDS

In describing events only, we lose our chance to understand.

A slow motion bullet burns through the shirt, pierces the skin, and enters the chest, sending him backwards, then folding him to the ground. The yells and screams of comrades, the crackling of enemy fire, the acrid smell of smoke, all fade into a dark night of forever.

* * *

We watched it on tv nightly—a war brought inside. Only here the battlefield was Ohio, our town, our streets, as students were turned back with a volley of shots that tore open everything. The bell that had been rung to assemble that day now tolled for the four who had been lost, the dozen wounded by bullets, the others by the violence of brother fighting brother.

* * *

I was at home while my daughter slept inside. Our neighbor came out on the porch crying. "Larry, they're shooting our students." We stood in the sound of it. It made no sense then or now. We listened to the radio, the reports, the rumors burning us with fear and hatred. *"It has been reported that four National Guardsmen have been wounded on the campus of Kent State University in Ohio."* The phone rang. It was Ann calling from Robinson Memorial Hospital to see if we were okay. "I can't believe it," she sighed, then "The radio has it all wrong. It's all students we have here. They're bringing them in dead and wounded on stretchers. You guys stay where you are. Okay? I'll be home as soon as I can get off here." "Come the back roads," I said. "I love you."

* * *

When Laura awakened, I was still sitting there mute. For an hour I watched her sweet face watching *Sesame Street*. Rose had gone home to her son coming home from school. The night before, we had all stood out front, watching the smoke of ROTC buildings rise over the campus. We had talked of what it all meant, the second night of rioting against the war. This night we would be kept awake by our thoughts and by the thick sound of helicopters circling overhead—thunk, thunk, thunk, thunk, thunk. We held each other close and worried a future for us and our child.

*   *   *

Our campus was placed under martial law. The students I had been teaching were vanished to their homes. One wrote me, "My father said he was glad they had shot them. They were destroying property. When I told him I had been on the hill that day watching, he said, 'Well maybe you should have been shot.'" After a week I was allowed an hour to get my books. The news settled into facts, but it was still the story of a babbling child. What meaning can be read from the death of innocents? How do we explain the flowering of loss inside our chest, the poison inside our blood?

*   *   *

The next year we had moved north to a house by the lake, to new jobs teaching and nursing. Laura started school down the street. Many of my students were returning veterans who spoke against the war. Yet the battles raged, despite our protests. We spoke of Kent State only with each other, mourning alone the loss of America.

THE WRITING LIFE

Reasons:

It is who I am. I can't stop writing any more than I can stop breathing, this need to connect, to build something in the dark, to listen close and make out of it, to repair a broken world, calm an aching heart, to witness in story and image, to find a path by making one, to surprise myself. It is who I am.

The Publishing:

The first publication gives your work validation, something that you eventually learn only you can give when you're being true to the experience, the language, yourself.

And so I read my own writing—with care, feeling the words go down talking to each other, finding a path, building something out of air: emotion, thought, senses, knowings.

My father worked with his hands. I build this way.

Tearing down our vanity is a long career. Eventually we begin to see what it does and doesn't mean.

We all have our gifts. Writing must be given away. With skill and time we learn to use and not abuse it.

If we stay at it, the words and pages, the magazines and books, all of it builds up as though it were something, something that seems to exist, and yet each time we pick up the pen or begin to type, we know it is all dust, and knowing this, believing it, we begin again.

THE STORIES OF LOVE

I am licking the stamps from your hands and remembering the rain. Your hair and your eyes move the same.

*　　　*　　　*

And she told you I cared and you knew he was my friend so I gave it to him but for you and we met on the stairs going up and down yet we laughed together going out the door.

*　　　*　　　*

When I saw your face I wanted more. In the car against the snow we learned to dance in each other's touch. It was like making birds, like baking memories. When you cried I couldn't breathe, and I opened the window on myself.

*　　　*　　　*

On the phone you sounded strangely new and I too had been turning. I thought of death and feared the other side. When we touched again it was bread rising on the bed. It was morning, and the new of this day had just arrived.

*　　　*　　　*

Sometimes I lie open on the bed dreaming of your ways. And there are days when you lie beside me and we kiss the age we've made. And sometimes when I'm holding you holding me I begin to learn how to die.

THE STORY OF MARRIAGE

Trees grow in the space between us.
We touch them when we have time.

All day you have been turned looking at the stones within.
And I have been watching you like a fish.

Comes a time and you are watching me digging holes in the sand.
And between us lies the sea where the birds are thick with silence.

In the night falls a seed beside us. We pick it together the next day.
It opens to the songs of children laughing.

The sky falls each day, they say.
Only some days we catch it in our arms.

THE HAIRCUT STORY

My son needs his hair cut and so do I. He has a special barber that he goes to, an older man like my father who gave haircuts to me. I have another barber who cuts mine.

I can't cut hair; only once did I trim the back of my father's neck which he couldn't cut in a mirror. So I put a hat and gloves on my son and we head for the barbershop.

It is closed. The candy cane sign isn't turning, and it looks like night in there. I tell him we will go to my barber to get his hair cut. He says no, he doesn't want to. I tell him he will. He says that I need a haircut too. I agree. I do. And so we drive.

Walking from the car to the barber's he puts his hand in mine, and we notice puddles from last night's rain. Bird footprints trim the edge. He thinks this is very funny, like a drawing inside a photograph. I laugh.

At the barbershop (only one customer inside), I hold the door for him and we can feel the light and heat inside. We enter the little room.

There in the chair is his barber staring up at us, first at me and then my son. His eyes want to know what we are doing there. We stare back at him like mirrors. My son looks up to ask which barbershop is this. My barber says hello, you're next; the other barber nods. My barber is done cutting now and he won't let the other barber pay. My son's barber insists; the other barber says no, it's a professional courtesy, someday you'll do the same for me.

He cuts both our hair. First my son, and then me.

A PIECE BROKEN OFF

A boy comes to our house each morning to tell us where he has been. He stands at the front door while snowflakes fill his eyes, and he talks about his travels and the persons that are him. I stand in my robe and listen to this face that mirrors mine. I want to give him food or have him in, but he can't stop talking for me to begin. Soon my wife is there listening and loving every word. His voice is like weather; his words are dice coming up through milk. He never stops, just turns and walks, and lets the day begin.

THINGS MY FATHER TAUGHT ME

Wakened by his footsteps, as he dressed in morning dark, I'd lie there
waiting his call to rise and shine. He moved with purpose, like the
railroad. His hands wore the callouses of work; his eyes were dark
pools of trust. He taught with what he was, with words like apples
sweet and tart—

> Trust the road that takes you.
>> Let the saw do its work.
>>> The worst fear is fear of work.
>>> Let the shovel throw the dirt.
>>> Enjoy the work you do, and the job will answer back.
>> Let the hammer drive the nail.

Drawn down into his basement where our hair was cut, my brother
and I sat around his heavy workbench waiting his words of manhood.
We grinned to see him blush, looked away to his drills and saws as he
spoke simply from his life–

> Women are there to be cared for. Love them as yourself.
>> The wrong you make goes on until you claim it.
>> Family blood extends to everyone.
> When you speak ill of another, you speak ill of yourself.

And from the father who never struck me, who seldom touched me,
whose knuckles were Boy Scout knots, whose muscled arms were
tools–
> When you begin to lie, you start to sell yourself.
>> Hold the word that hurts.
>>> Don't confuse your wants with your needs.
>>> Kindness speaks through silence.

This year I wear his hat, feel his touch inside this coat. Inside my voice
he speaks of what it means to be. He loved with what he was.

CUTTING DOWN THE MAPLE
IN MY FATHER'S YARD

for my father

It is the day after Thanksgiving, and we walk out in morning air. The leaves have already gone, and my father is showing me how the bark has come away from the trunk. It clearly can't be saved. So we bring ladders up from the garage, my brother's chainsaw out from the basement.

As I hold this ladder for my father, my son runs about the yard chasing their old dog, and there is this unspeakable sadness. I see it is a 62-year-old man up there cutting branches which fall at my feet. Why do I allow him to do it? Because I want him young, and yet I fear his loss. I am on the ladder myself holding him.

My father offers me the noisy saw. I shy away. *No, go ahead and cut*, I say. He holds it out again and nods, *You'll need to know this soon enough*. But I let him cut. *I'll gather up*, I say, and I remember all the times I've worked with him, the lights and tools I've handed over. I've come to love his act of work, the surest thing I know.

I catch the logs as they fall from his saw and stack them near the garage. My son drags the thin branches down the yard. And soon our arms grow warm with work. There is no need to talk. We speak in acts, the light inside the yard.

In the sunny rhythm of our working I think...How did this man, my father, become so easily old? I want my son to know this man. I want this job to never end. I will ache for weeks with the rightness of this work.

SEASON OF SICILY

For a year our ground was the earth of Italy, the Sicilian lava coast at the foot of Mt. Etna. Our air was that of sea and mountain, seacoast and city. We gave up our Ohio place for a taste of Sicily—its pizza and coffee, its pastry and bitter oranges, its hundred pastas, its dark and friendly people—all for the chance to grow in another land. Our American faces and walk, our blond and blue-eyed children earned us local attention, disdain, and finally acceptance. I took a flat tire from our old leased Fiat to the *gumisti* man, and he wrote on the rim, "*Americano.*"

The older children rode off to school, and I walked Suzanne to the maternity school each day, past the lizards and cactus plants, and I smiled to everyone, the old women in black standing in their doorways, the busy shopkeepers, the women out on the corner buying from the fish man. And I too would consider the fish, point out a dozen little ones to fillet and fry up for dinner that night. The larger ones, he cut for me, and the women would argue for their heads for soup. Ann would be making beds or hanging clothes to dry on the porch. The sun touched everything, even us.

At the university I was "*professore,*" the *Americano* come to teach of Whitman and Thoreau, Kerouac and Ginsberg. I parked along the wall and stopped at the little café, drank a morning espresso standing up, then strolled into the old building, my mind full of light. I would sit in my office, the American library, read and wait for students. Classes never started on time; our books never arrived; I had to bribe the xerox man, but I was *professore.*

The Fulbright Foundation paid us just enough to survive and no more, and though waiters and shop owners thought we were rich American tourists, the people of *Aci Castello* came to know us as common. We were fine with that; we craved their acceptance, a family to belong to, a neighborhood to join. After months of struggling, we were able to speak with them, use their words to name their world. Hear their ways.

Yes, it was beautiful and unforgettable, the Sicilian year—1980-1981; we still date from before and after that time. But, like the sea and weather, it was not easy; it was a struggle that bound us as family, a battle to endure without and yet provide. My dreams were haunted by fears of losing them at train stations, into the sea, out on the road.

One day after months of living there, while riding the bus to Syracusa, the driver began playing music, John Denver's "Country Roads, Take Me Home..." I could not take my hand from my son's palm to wipe away my tears.

Before we returned, we had found Ann's Italian family in *Giulianova*, held them and ate together with them on the farm trading family stories; we had made a hundred friends of our Italian neighbors; learned more than we could ever teach; then we came home to America and our trusting families who hugged us at the airport and let us feel our way back home in their homes. It took weeks, months, to assimilate again. So much could not translate. We had tasted the goodness of bread, the warmth of sun, the touch of a people as strong as their land. We had found our own strength and survived.

When people ask us how it was, we smile to each other still and say, "Just grand."

THE COMPANY OF WIDOWS

Every couple of months or so I return to the industrial Ohio Valley with its deep green Appalachian walls along that big winding river. And lately as I come into town bouncing over the gaping potholes of Steubenville streets, stopping at the traffic light beside that huge bridge to West Virginia, I stare at the new monument to the steel valley, a statue of a laborer in shiny asbestos suit frozen at that moment when he taps a sample from the blast furnace floor. He seems intent upon his job, only there is no blast furnace floor, just this laborer alone in time and space. I admire the statue's simple directness, its human scale and respect for reality. For me, this whole steel valley remains as real and fluid as the hot flowing iron of memory.

As I round the curve under the Market Street Bridge, my windows down to make a summer breeze, there is that aftertaste of something burnt in the air, and I swear you can taste it too in the water, as bittersweet as rust. Heavy barges of coal and ore move down river beside me as the gray air billows from smokestacks, rises and crests in a dark heavy cloud. I am enough of an outsider now to notice this; insiders never do, or if it gets too heavy and they are forced to cough each time they speak, they blame it on the milltown across the river— "Smells like Follansbee!" This place along the edge, so marked by extremes of beauty and waste, is my place, my hometown, my family—and I breathe and swallow it again.

"It ain't all bad," as they say, and I look over to see my wife awake now as we come into "Mingo Town." She smiles too at being home; my son looks up from his computer game at the blast furnaces that loom over the town, and we wake our twelve year old daughter, who asks, "Are we at Grandma's yet?"

I smile as the car winds up the steep hill, and pulls in before a yellow brick home. I unload our bags and leave everyone at Ann's mother's, then drive down St. Clair hill, staring into the steaming cauldrons of the mill. At Murdock Street I turn right, coast downhill, and pull in behind my mother's car. She has taken down the front maple, leafless for years, so that the whole place looks a little different and a whole lot the same; a three-story wooden frame house with worn green shingles along the edge of Ohio Route 7.

Mrs. Maul nods to me as I get out—neighbors still, her yard still cared for like her retarded son who is now 33 and staring out the window at me. I wave then note how Mom's porch needs the mill dirt squirted off. I take the broom by the door, and start dancing it across the green painted concrete till she hears me, comes to the front window laughing, "Get in here, you nut."

It is at least a five minute wait as she wrestles her door locks, three of them where once there were none. But I don't object, I want her safe, and with the recent break-ins and thefts from cars, I tell her I will install another if she wants. "Don't worry," she says hugging me home, "We old girls keep an eye out for each other."

In Mom's house one never gets further than the "television room" where the set is always on. I've found her sleeping here some nights in her reclining chair in the glow of a snowy screen. We sit and she gives me news of who has died or been arrested, and word of my lost siblings; she offers me candy and a glass of root beer. She is sixty-four this year, my father's fatal heart attack upstairs, now three years past. Though we often speak of him, of what he'd think, of how he used to work so hard, of his joking with the kids, we never address his death. We both know that he is gone—the whole house echoes his absence, but we won't recall for each other those weeks around his death when we went through his things, sorting out tolls and clothes, taking papers from the mill to the social security office in Steubenville. It still breaks my heart remembering my mother sitting in that office, hearing her say to the stranger, "My husband's dead, now what do I do?"

Only this time as she brings in a plate of store-bought cookies, I am surprised to hear her say, "That day your dad died, he took a handful of these and a glass of milk. I remember, he said he was just going upstairs to lie down. He said he had to rest."

I cannot breathe for the weight of this, something caught in my own chest which somehow asks, "Mom, what happened that day Dad died? Who found him, did you?"

Our eyes just touch before she goes to sit, "Oh, yes, it was me that found him—here in our bed, asleep I thought at first, yet somehow I knew." She takes a breath as the scene begins, "He'd come home from golfing with his buddies saying that his arm was hurting. He started golfing several times a week since the mill retired him." Her eyes look distant as she talks, like she's watching all this on a television screen somewhere. "I called to him, touched his arm, and he felt cold lying there. God I was scared, so I called Darlene and she called the emergency squad. They got here quick. His friend Brownie was with them. He's the one came downstairs to tell me, 'Jeanny,' he said, 'there's nothing more we can do—' I remember him standing right here where you are, saying that. 'There's nothing more we can do,'" and she sighs. "Brownie's a good old boy, been your father's friend since they were school boys."

"Was there a doctor who came?" I have to ask.

"No, just the paramedics, but then they took him straight to the hospital where he was pronounced dead." Suddenly she looks at me as though she has awakened out of a trance and is waiting for me to explain.

Only I can't. All I can say is, "It must have been hard for you. I'm sorry I wasn't around." There is a silence between us so still that we notice the hoot and crash of the mill as the trains take a haul of slag down to the pits. The mill is always there in this town—in the sounds and smells, the color of the air and in the talk—"What they got you workin', midnight?" "We'd come up, but Michael's workin' four-to-twelve next month...." Work is the fabric of life here.

Married at eighteen, my father worked as a brakeman on the railroad at Weirton Steel for forty years, till they forced him to retire. All this is *there* inside the room-his awareness of a life

"How'd you get through it all, Mom?"

"Well, Darlene was here, and your sister Debbie had come down by then. I think Dr. Ruksha came by and gave me something. I can't remember now. Debbie would."

There's another long silence as we think about all that's just been said. This is further than we've ever gone into it, the gritty details of a death, and it's almost as though we've stirred up a part of ourselves we thought was dead. I smile at her, "How come we never talked about this, Mom?"

She looks back, "I don't know." And then she thinks to say, "I know he's gone—Lord how I miss that old boy—but he's still here inside this house. You know, I can feel him sometimes. I think I hear him calling up from the basement, 'Honey, where's my work clothes?' or some such thing. I almost answer him, then I stop." She smiles quietly, "I guess I'm losing touch. But you know, I always feel better when I think of him, like having him back in a dream."

I go over and hug her in her chair, and we can both sense the grief in each other. "What does it all mean?" she sighs, and I just hold her, so frail and quiet.

"You did all you could, Mom. All anyone can."

Now it is I who have to move about, so I walk out into the kitchen for a drink. The radio is playing the area talk show—'Will the schools be forced to consolidate if the mills don't pay back taxes?' It is a mix of local gossip and preparing for the worst. My wife's uncle talks of retiring at forty-five. "What do I care?" he asks, "I can't let the mills decide my life. What's going to happen anyway, when it all shuts down? Have you thought of that?" And he shakes his head sitting on his front porch, "Who owns these mills? Who decides what happens here?" I shake my own head. "We steelmakers are a forgotten race," he concludes and I have no more answer for him than for my mother in the other room.

I could tell her of my own dreams of my father—of how he appeared in our house, smiling and tried to tell me a joke I couldn't get-how he laughed as if to say he was okay now. I know I felt good for a week, but dreams fade quicker than memories. Back in this valley the struggle toughens you or it breaks your heart. And where do you draw the line?

I think of how my father didn't complain of his arm or chest on the day he died, and wonder if he might not be alive if he had. But, wasn't he trained here not to feel the pain, not to complain? Pouring my coffee, measuring my cream, I wonder how much we give up to survive? How much did my father?

I stir it together and I know these are futile questions, yet somewhere I've learned that ignoring a truth creates another sort of pain and a kind of blind numbness around the heart. I remember how Dad, scoutmaster of my youth, would stop our car on the street to break up a kids' fight; he couldn't let a wrong go on. His working so hard, sending two boys through college, may have been his own way of rebelling against a silent lie. I take a drink of valley coffee and sit back down on the couch.

While my mother goes to take her medication I leaf through the local *Herald Star*. When she returns I ask, "Mom, what's this parade they're having uptown in Steubenville today—Festival Homecoming? Do you want to go?"

She smiles, "Sure, when is it?" Like a child now she welcomes small adventures and a chance for company. I know that kitchen radio is her best friend most days, that's why I bought it for her, and to quell my own guilt for moving away to my quiet home along the lake.

"They say at 2:00, but there's already a street fair on Fourth and Market if you want to take that in. Have you seen it?"

"Debbie and Michael took Robin the other night," as she sits. "They said she rode a pony in the street. I can't imagine that. A pony in the middle of Market Street that used to be so busy with traffic."

"Yeah," I say, and we both know the story of how the old downtown of Steubenville died four years ago after the layoffs, then again with the opening of the Fort Steuben Shopping Mall. And we both secretly wish we could be wrong about this, that the town will yet survive. Somehow our valley toughness doesn't exclude a capacity to dream.

At noon I show up again having retrieved my wife, son and daughter. My mother-in-law Sue has joined us in this summer thirst for a celebration. A widow like Mom, Sue carries her John with her all the time. Instead of wearing a widow's black, she refused to smile for a year and a half. She's a strong Italian woman whose fierce integrity and hard work make her a legend in her neighborhood. John too did his 40 years in the mills, as a millwright—humble and happy on his job till they took it from him claiming his eyes were too weak. They were weak but twice as strong as the benefits the mill paid for his "early out." And while I know these forced retirements didn't kill our dads, I curse the thoughtless pain they brought to good people. Sue works now in the school cafeteria—baking cookies and cakes, fish and french fries for a troop of teenagers. They give her a hard time but love her cooking. They always ask whether she cooked it before they buy...she is seventy.

My wife Ann and daughter Suzanne are like her in their strong will. In the Valley you learn early, if you learn at all, that work and self-belief are your strongest tools. My mother-in-law's favorite saying, besides "The rich get richer, and the poor get poorer" and "At least we eat good," is... "Well we have each other."

Ann offers the front seat to my mother, but she refuses, climbing into the back–"No, no, we belong back here. Don't we, Sue? The merry widows and Suzanne." We all laugh, as Ann and Brian squeeze together; they begin to talk as I cruise up river to the celebration, to the hope a parade brings.

As we enter town from the North I search for a parking place— up close and free. I must prove to all these women that they haven't a fool for a son, husband or father.

Finally, we pull onto the hot asphalt of the city lot, and I feed dimes to the meter. We cross the light down Adams to the street fair. The parade will follow these outside streets and march a square around the intersection of Fourth and Market. It's a good thing too, as those two streets are packed with noisy citizens barking back at the game keepers, standing in line for rides, or wolfing down Italian sausage and onions with a sudsy Budweiser in the afternoon. The whole street smells like a local bar, and there is hardly room to pass as we bump good naturedly into our neighbors. A flow in this human river, pushed on, I almost lose my wife who waves a hand above the heads. We laugh on the street corner, "So many people," I say, and she adds, "And we actually know some of them," an inside joke to small-town emigrants living in anonymous suburbs where the faces seem familiar yet you know none of them.

As a rock band blasts and rumbles from the flatbed of a truck, we feel at "home." And though we know this busy downtown street will become a deserted crime area again come Monday, for a while, our memory is washed by the flood of our senses.

Sue tells Ann to tell me that it's time to find a place to watch the parade, and so I look around then lead us back from Washington Street, only this time along the sidewalk, past the back of the Italian and Irish booths smelling of spaghetti and corned beef with nearly matching flags, past the abandoned J. C. Penney's building, the closed furniture and clothing stores—so empty full of darkness—past the Slovak church's pirogi and raffle booth, to the corner of Fourth and Adams.

The old Capital Theatre has been leveled to build a store to sell tires and auto parts. It's been gone for years, but each time it hits me with its large sense of absence. In fact I realize that I have been vibrating with this same sense of presence and absence since we arrived. Struck by the sense of what is here and what is not, I struggle to assimilate the change.

In the midst of parents pushing their children toward a noisy, street merry-go-round, I recall how my wife and I once sat close together in the cushioned seats of the Capital Theatre while Tony and Maria of *West Side Story* sang so desperately of their love struggle. It was the first time we kissed. Perhaps my whole little family really began in search of such close moments? Perhaps. What I do know is that things change even in this old town. Facing that, I know my real problem is understanding the direction of that change.

Waiting here on the curb along the corner, I've been noticing things. Not just the noise and vacant stores but the changed sense of the place. What has survived and how? The angry fumes of the One-Hour Dry Cleaners still spill out onto the street and I remember its sickening smell and sticky feel as I picked up a suit standing there forced to breathe it as I watched the weary movement of the women at their mangles, caught the hurried tone of the clerks. And of course the bars are still here, one for every third storefront, and the Sports & Cigar places not driven out by the legal lottery. One bakery is still open, reminding me of time spent waiting for the bus breathing the hearty bread and donut smells till I had to purchase "Just one, please," from the Downtown Bakery. All the Five and Dime stores have been converted to self-serve drugstores, the restaurants to offices or video rentals, the clothing stores empty as night.

I stand there making this mental documentary when my daughter insists, "Dad, I'm hungry." We adults suddenly look to each other and realize she is right, we have forgotten lunch. I look back to the booths, then back at my son who is pointing down Adams Street; we smile, one of the brightest moments of the day, for we are a half block away from one of the best pizza shops in Ohio, perhaps the world.

"I'll be back in a minute," I tell them, and take my daughter's hand and follow Brian down the street to DiCarlo's Italian Pizza. Inside, the mixed aromas of Parmesan cheese, warm dough, spicy pepperoni and sauce bring me back. It is a Roman pizza they make, sold by the square, and the crust is crisp yet chewy with juicy chunks of tomato melting into the mozzarella cheese and pepperoni which they throw on last like scattered seed. I point this out to my child, all the while remembering those years of standing at this same counter watching the rich ritual of the men tossing dough hard on counters, of their moving the pizza up the oven drawers as it rose steadily to a climax, cut and boxed, a rubber band snapped around the corners, the holes popped to keep it crisp. We buy two dozen and hurry back to our crowd, to that first bite into the steaming slab, chewing it well, a piece at a time. And it's good to taste how some things stay the same.

Standing as we eat, I notice the need for napkins, to catch the dripping but also to keep it clean from all the street dirt blowing along the curb. "It's a shame," Sue clucks, nodding to the way litter lies along the street—not just cigarette butts, though there are plenty of those, but whole bags from Burger King, empty pop and beer cans that the residents step over, like hard stones on the sidewalk. "The city levy didn't pass," I am told, and I nod as if I understand, but it is all wrong.

Like watching your child pulled from a sports game, I am really torn that what seems so precious to me feels so easily abused. Yet I check my sense of righteous-ness knowing how much I've moved away from here, to my suburban life, a college teaching job, a safe haven along Lake Erie. I do not wish to accent my estrangement. I eat my pizza with my son on the curb.

People begin lining the curbs standing or seated in their lawn chairs. They stand and talk or occasionally watch up the street for the start of things. The police walk by us, a kid waits then darts across the street. Something is about to begin. Watching the faces of people standing near me I look for the familiar but find only the strange…a woman in a POISON T-shirt yanking her child up by the arm smacking her really hard on the butt, screaming "I told you to pee before we left!" this time with a smack to the face, "Didn't I?" No one says anything. "Well, didn't I?" The child only wails while the mother bellows, "Now, you run home, Missy, and change those pants. You'll miss the parade." The straw haired woman seems oblivious to all around her, as though the street is her home. This is something our parents and neighbors never did, no dirty laundry aired in the street. Her husband joins her now on stage and, yes, he is a hairy guy with those dark blue tattoos flaming up and down his arms. He brushes by her. "Hey, Babe, I'm goin' for a beer!" falls off his lips like spit, as he pushes his way through the crowd. "Oh, no you're not!" she shouts at him. "You're not leaving me again with these kids!" And it seems her whole life *is a* series of exclamations as she walks off leaving her children at our feet. They don't seem to notice, and most of the crowd looks back up the street trained now at ignoring these small unforgivable scenes of communal violence.

It is my mother-in-law who hisses, *"Sceevo"* and folds her pizza away in her napkin. It's an Italian expression, a succinct verb that means, "It makes me sick," and I know it is not the pizza but the mean ugliness that has repulsed her. It haunts the streets as I look hard at the faces in the crowd of locals who seem as strangely foreign to me as the news from Iraq. It's like watching the films made in this area—Michael Cimino's *The Deer Hunter*, or Peter Strauss' *Hearts of Steel*. The setting is right but the people are all wrong—not because they are actors but because they are portraying the valley and its people at their most desperate to preach Hollywood despair or false hope. That film *life* feels close yet alien to anyone who knows this place, a twin hurt that confuses me like these wounded faces around me. They are not the faces I grew up with here, those who lived well though poor and somehow shared the good that they had and were.

As I watch this woman turn back, I try to feel her life, guess her age, but it is impossible—the facial lines and cold eyes, the young children at our feet. She turns to us, motions to her kids, yells to my puzzled mother, "I'll be right back!" And so we find ourselves baby-sitting her girls on the street comer. The children take no notice until we offer them a pizza which they grab and gobble down, thanking us with their eyes. It's a sad scene, and this human gesture seems the only way to dispel the curse of this family's life. I need to understand.

"Mom," I turn to ask her, "Do you know these people?"

"Oh, no, I don't know her," she says, then realizes what I've asked. "There's a new crowd that lives downtown now."

"Where did they come from?" I hear myself ask.

She answers, "When everyone started moving out of downtown, they started moving in." She gestures broadly to the old buildings across the street, and I see above the storefronts, the backs of buildings, windows with ragged curtains, bags of trash out in the street beside junked cars. And my heart sags like the dirty clouds or this child's heavy diaper.

Sue adds, "Apartments are cheap now, cause nobody wants to live where so many muggings go on." She goes on to report the worst and most recent incidents while I wonder which came first—the crime or the abandonment. She can't help telling these stories, because it has happened to her friends; it's a part of her life now. She plays out her old storyteller's hand—hoping by telling to somehow understand.

And I think of another conversation last week with a city planner now working as a car salesman. "No jobs for city planners," he jokes. So when I tell him of my dismay at understanding the way cities change, he describes for me the 'myth of urban renewal.' "See, they throw up a few new office buildings that look good to the outsiders. Right?" I remember nodding. "Only what you don't see is also what you get. To the city poor it means something else—less and worse housing. Where do you think all the 'homeless' people come from?" he asks while downing a half cup of coffee. "I'll tell you. Urban renewal drives some of them into the street and it drives a lot of others away to smaller cities like your hometown where they have no support, sense of past and no hope of a future. And so there they live unconnected, and just using up the present."

I had nothing more to say to him or now to myself as this parade begins. I just stand here thinking: of the fathers who worked this valley farming labor into families along the river land, and of the widows now forced to watch the rich soil used up, spoiled by greed and unconcern. I know that my father had no answer for this either, and for once I am glad he doesn't have to be here to watch it all happen. I just stare across the street at an older man tending cars in the parking lot. He moves aimlessly from car to car, checking tags, and I recognize something in his face. My mother whispers his name, a classmate of mine, his face a shadow of my own.

Held there on the curb of the Steubenville street that feels so close yet strange, I become my own mute statue.

As the parade goes by, I watch how the faces light up at so little. The children are smiling at a clown squirting water from his motorcycle. A float of Junior Women toss candy at our feet. My mother waves to friends. I find myself nodding to everyone, yet inside myself I am thinking of the five words given to me by my ex-city planner: "Abandonment creates its own culture." It sums up my own confused pain now, and I say it over and over to myself, "Abandonment creates its own culture." In the summer heat, the parade passes, we smile into late afternoon sun, and then we take the widows home.

THE VISIT

for Bob

Toward the end of summer, when all the grass is brown, a rain will come. My friend has driven up from Columbus, to play guitar and spend the night. We sit outside in lake wind and talk of family and jobs, of houses and dogs.

The branches of the maple sway like dancing arms.

He tells me how he tries to be home when his daughter comes from school. I talk with mine on long college drives. His son wants to move out; mine to get married. Last time we spoke of the male hair grown upon their legs.

Birds flit through trees; the dog barks to join us.

At fifty, our fathers gone, we each hold the rudder through seas strange and dark. "Some days at work," he sighs, "I feel almost overwhelmed." Born a week apart, we have always spoken for each other.

The magnolia tree shades our afternoon beers
as a cat walks through the yard.

I tell him how lonely it seems without parents, and he nods. "If it weren't for Ann," I say, "it would be impossible."
"I know," he smiles across the afternoon.

Above the house comes the soft hoot of mourning doves predicting rain. He takes his guitar in hand and walks us down an old blues tune. We both lean forward into it, knowing the melody of pain.

Soon evening will come and we will go to eat inside. For now his music is enough for anyone who hears.

APPALACHIAN SUNRISE

for Suzanne

The sun rises over the hills as I step out onto the porch of my daughter's college house.

A few starlings dart in and out of the tall bushes. The housemates all asleep inside, each in their nest while weekend trash climbs the walls outside.

The air is cool and musty here in the shadow-light of trees as silent as the coal mines closed for years. A beer can rolls along an alley; a yellow cat cuddles inside the window.

Soon my daughter will rise to shower with morning.

Last night on her bed she sat beside her mother and me saying, "I love having you here," and we laughed with the knowing, with being so near her garden where the growth is clear.

We have each come a long way to be where we are. I sip my coffee and breathe slow. Inside she sleeps softly, and I sit on her front porch couch blinded with light.

FAMILY WITH CHILD

for Laura, Allen, and Rosa

Lying on your futon, daughter, I look out at gray Seattle skies.
Dark birds glide by and land on wet telephone lines.

From the kitchen comes the smell of dark Seattle coffee—
your mother up and showered from our night of talk and love.

Upstairs you and Allen nestled with your baby Rosa, flowers
all of you in a bed.

We have all come so far to be here in morning light.

Your baby, your banjo, your books, your candles and strings
of lights. Your feet upon the stairs, Baby Rosa wrapped in your
arms. Your soft hair and eyes. This place where we all live.

SUNDAY MORNINGS: ADDRESSING MY RELIGION

I sit at mass in my wife's religion, and while others take communion, I lean back, remember long ago in my father's church, hearing the choir warble hymns, standing between him and my brother, eyeing the bare faced girls in the choir. Once I asked God to give me a sign, then sweated in fear that he would. I went off to college, sat in chapel twice a week and church on Sunday, our attendance monitored by upperclassmen, hearing the deep boom of the pipe organ, the ringing choir of voices, thinking to myself: *So this is religion!*—nearing it, fearing it, asking whose right to define a love so common and divine. I lean back against the wooden bench now, watch the faces of the others through the sound of prayer.

*　　*　　*

On my back porch, watching black-throated sparrows take over the feeder; the tiny wren makes a huge warble that a new house has been found. A chipmunk joins a mourning dove gathering the fallen seed. Each finds his share.

*　　*　　*

A young woman sits beneath the leaves doing yoga stretches, telling us to relax, lie back, let go; to reach out, breathe deep into ourselves, ride it through the pain. Her voice is a caring flute, her form glides tenderly in space. And I do come into myself, the one inside who waits and watches without thought, the one grown strong and fair, who shares the common air.

*　　*　　*

Lying beside her, I kiss her hair on summer sheets as she hums softly a music of our touch. This love is God's testing and reward, the one brought into the self, the self shared with the other on a journey longer than time and space. Her eyes press a kiss, I tremble at the sound of rain falling around us, the church of our bodies.

*　　*　　*

I sit in meditation posture at Zen Mountain Center as the day gives itself to evening. Breathing through the pain of old knees and aching back, counting moments as the birds warble outside the temple windows. The rich smell of incense through time, the deep gong for rest moving us to slowly rise, walk briskly around the room. This is a mute Quakers' meeting, a festival of silence as we all feel the stillness grow. I drift and come back, fall through paper self into the fiber of oneness, the web of connectedness, the sea of meaning. I will walk out from here into the night woods, find my way back by listening close, walk the river home. I become again the one who watches without knowing, the one who swims through to rise again.

*　　*　　*

I sit in the town diner, reading the faces of others, listening to the murmur of their voices over coffee and eggs. The waitress rolls her dark hair into a ponytail, counts us with her eyes, stands and waits our wishes. She has fine dark eyes already tired from figuring, remembering. I too count the soft moments between, learn to enjoy the waiting.

New faces enter and nod to the waitress who escorts them in as she carries us our food. We all smile as they pass, then eat our food as though it were the first and last.

THE STUDENTS THIS YEAR

All day I have been teaching without a rest, until a young woman reads to the class her essay of being raped. Her soft eyes are full of pain and courage, and she does not cry until I say, "You're very brave."

Monday I am preparing for classes when a woman knocks at my office door. She begins to introduce herself as one of my students; I say, "I know you." And her eyes finally look up frightened and ashamed. She says her paper will be late because she cannot think. In what seems a breath, she tells me her husband of 19 years has left her.

I say, "That must be hard." And she, "It's for the best. I see that now. He's abused me for 20 years."

Silence flows between us as she looks away, "I see it now in my oldest boy." She winces away tears, "I'm small. It doesn't take much." Her voice quivers like a struck animal as she sighs, "I've got to protect my youngest boy."

We are two people caught in reality's harsh light. I tell her there are places and people who might help her, but she rises, slowly, her body already weighted down. I want to touch her hair as a daughter but say instead, "Do the paper when you can. Take care of yourself."

Today, she dropped my course.

*   *   *

This year I have heard the stories of so many: men whose plants closed down and who cannot swallow their own anger and scorn, women whose children are gone and who hope now to birth themselves. One lives in a camper with her two kids; another's hopes lie with her disability.

*   *   *

In class last week I ask, "How many know someone without health insurance?"

Ten nod—"Yeah, *me*." Young faces of those who hope someday to do almost as well as their parents.

I tell one boy he is missing too many classes and will fail. He looks into my grave face and smiles, "Hey, man. It's okay, really," then disappears around the corner.

*   *   *

Yesterday a woman called to say "I'm having trouble with my son. His father wants to steal him back. I can't leave him to come to class." And I can only think to say "I'll see you when you can," then add, "Take care..."

*   *   *

Today I show a film on the homeless and ask the class what they think. Slowly a woman rises to tell her story of living in a car for a year, of reading her way back from jail, of writing her way home here now.

*   *   *

This year my jokes about run-on sentences and punctuation as little road signs seem hollow before their lives. Out the window I watch as hundreds of starlings and sparrows cluster on the ground and trees; I hope they are finding food.

This fall I hear their stories and wonder who could not love them.

Ann (Zaben) Smith graduation
Wheeling Hospital, 1965

Larry's college gratuation
Muskingum College, 1965

Ann and Larry
wedding photo
St. Agnes Catholic
Church, Mingo
Junction, 1965

Infant Laura with Larry
Euclid, Ohio 1967

Brian, Suzanne, Sue & John Zaben,
& Laura at their Mingo home, 1976

Weirton Steel Mill, blast furnace alley where father worked on railroad and Larry labored summers of 1964 & 1965

Tom Koba & Larry Smith, Wheeling-Pitt Steel Mill, Mingo, filming *James Wright's Ohio* 1988 (photo by Paul Ferguson)

Larry & Ann at Ponte Vecchio,
Florence, Italy 1981

Smith family in Syracusa, Sicily, 1981

Wheeling-Pitt Mills in Steubenville

Mother Jean at Larry's birthplace, Mingo

Larry & Jean, 1992

Laura, Allen, Rosa, Larry, Suzanne, Ann, Brian, Anna
Smith family in Huron, Ohio 1999

Smith siblings, David, Janis, Debbie, & Larry
Poland, Ohio 1999

Larry & Ann, 1995   Ann, baby Adam, Larry 2000

Part III

(Photo © Connie Girard)

I have nothing to report my friends.
If you would know the way,
Stop chasing after so many things.

-Ryokan (*Kanshi Poems*)

SEASON OF CANCER

SHADOWS ON THE WATER

That's how it feels, knowing that your body carries cancer—
knowing that the shadow lies upon you, sinks beneath your skin.

And you ask yourself again how it entered and began.
What was it you did that let it in? And you try to image it,
a growth of cells that feeds upon your health.

Alone on a bank you cast stones through water and wait,
talk to your fears, feel how always is near. Who do you tell?
Who do you want to know so they can remind you that your
body eats itself? Their advice is a mirror of their lives.

I go out in the yard and cut the grass knowing, feeling my body
sweat as always, my back ache with turning. What has changed—
only the knowing and the still growth within.

I image a lump beneath the skin, knowing I will never swim again
with the same ease for distance. Yet swim I will, plunge inside the
water till it flows about and through me, hold onto nothing, nothing
I tell you. Letting go, to go on, inside the light and shadow.

WHAT YOU REALIZE WHEN CANCER COMES

You will not live forever—No, you will not, for a ceiling of clouds hovers in the sky.

You are not as brave as you once thought. Words of death echo in your chest.

You feel the bite of pain, the taste of it running through your veins.

Following the telling to friends comes a silence of felt goodbyes. You come to know the welling of tears.

Your children are stronger than you thought and closer to your skin.

The beauty of animals: birds on telephone lines, dogs who look into your eyes, all bring you peace.

You want no more confusion than what already rises in your head and heart.

You watch television less, will never read all those books, mark less the ones you have.

Songs can move you now, so that you want to hold onto the words like the hands of children.

Your own hands look good to you, old and familiar as water. You read your lover's skin, like a road map into yourself. All touch is precious now.

There are echoes in the words thrown before you. When they take your picture now, you wet your lips, swallow once, and truly smile.

Talk of your lost parents pulls you out, and brings you home again.

You are in a river, flowing in and through you.
Take a breath. Reach out your arms.
You can survive.

A river is flowing, flowing in and through you.
Take a breath. Reach out your arms.
You can survive.

TELLING AN OLD FRIEND

for Zita

I sit in the smalltown café with an old friend and tell her my cancer story—how they found it, what's been done, what choices are left to me—and she does not interrupt with advice or stories about other friends. Instead she nods and listens while I play this strange-sad music across our table above our glasses of water, our empty coffee cups. And when the waitress finally comes, we turn our minds to choices of eggs and toasts, decaf or regular. It is that pause between songs on a record or tape, and we're both wishing the new song will lift us above the mortality of words to visions and connections shared.

She begins telling me the story of her sixtieth birthday, spent among the Rockies. They had reached the highest point above the clouds and gotten out of their car. "Go on," Paul said, "I can't breathe so high," and she, afraid of heights, had climbed the last few yards to the peak, "I looked out...and knew that this was it—the top—below was snow, and below that the clustered towns with streets and cars."

It is I now who listens and waits as she smiles softly, "I'd spent my life climbing and could see now what was left to me." "I know,"I say, gesturing toward the wall, "I can sense now the way things begin and end."

We drink our coffees and spread jellies on our breads. I tell of a book I've finished, she of an exhibition of her art. It is food enough until we rise, hold each other close there in the late breakfast hour, then walk out together into light.

RESTING

My daughter stretches out beside me on her college bed, and whispers, "How are you doing?"

I tell her how the cancer grows in circles of dread, how I deal with it in waves of confrontation and fear. The bone scan waiting, the waking up to it each day.

She puts her head against my chest and we breathe softly, feel my old heart rest.

(Athens, Ohio, 9/28/97)

THE LIGHTING

My wife rolls over and says, "I think the furnace is dead." I go on reading in bed beside her.

The lamp goes out by itself, so I take off my glasses, lay them on the floor under the bed. An hour goes by while I think about things...the cost of a new furnace, where the kids are in their lives, the sound of the wind, the wind....

In my dream I am softly descending the stairs, carrying a candle down to the furnace. There is no sound or smell, as I bend over to look into its face. I do not like this furnace. It is not my friend but an old man who watches without words. I bring the candle up to see inside....A huge roar, then all is darkness...all is done.

I wake up shaking, struggling for air, see the room light through the darkness and try to lay there without waking Ann. I think of my father, a furnace man, who died suddenly while I was away. What would he say to me now? What have I to say to him?

My legs are feeling cold now, so I sit up, gather my glasses and walk into the hall. The thermostat is set at 70 degrees. The temperature is 58, my age. I must go down.

From the cupboard I take a flashlight and descend the cellar stairs...their creaking in the night, the dog's nails clicking down the steps behind me.

There is the furnace, cold and silent. I bend to look inside, see the pilot light is out. I turn the gas off and on again, smell the death it can bring.

I hold down the button, counting. Make each breath my first and last. Then reach down and light the match.

WALKING THROUGH

We wake before the sun arrives, before her mother starts coffee on her kitchen stove. Back in our old town we are guests at home, my wife and I, the woman I first kissed inside that kitchen door.

"Ready?" she asks and we are gone, dressed in winter warm. We pass beyond the houses climbing the steep hills dusted now with snow. The roar of the mill fades like a radio station.

In our fifties, we walk to keep alive, pump cool air into our lungs, an oxygen high. Yet this walking has a destination, a point on our trail. Trading stories we go up the hill, then down: an abandoned house there through trees, an old yellowed mining stream beside the road. Finally we climb through grass and gate to the cemetery gate and grounds, my parents' graves. Alone among neighbors' names they lie in peaceful air.

"Look," my wife calls— a moon through trees— a sun under clouds. Standing there over them in the fresh fog touching everything, I have no words

"Delbert and Jean Smith," I read aloud and begin raking with my hands under snow the leaves and weeds clustered at the marker's foot. A cold damp soils my skin and I am breathing hard with the weight of emotion held too long. No bird calls, only wind...

Suddenly my wife hugs my back and we lean together there, so that I can no longer speak aloud the greeting I would bring, but think it hard into the ground, "Mother, Father— I am coming towards you...Slowly towards you..."

Only my wife's arms warm me till we walk back into the life of this old and noisy town.

LIVING WITH IT

I live with a different fear now, that I might get well enough to die again some other way. It makes no sense and yet it does.

I had crossed the bridge over cancer, accepted its flow through me, and now I face the blank cold of the unknown. Of course I know the freedom this new cure brings, the release to play again.

Of course, I want to read the faces of my children forever and forever, yet know now how each cycle has its end. The faces of flowers open to it. The trees release their leaves to it. I have labored in rain and shadow to realize this, to claim its truth upon my skin.

And now I know, I must do so again.

RISING UP SHINING

My wife has already gone to work and I am drinking her sweetened coffee. I have taken my handful of pills, and as the dawn comes on I sit in my lounge chair reading the paper: The president's mess; welfare reform gone wrong; erosion of our lake shoreline; I feel helpless before it all. I hear the footsteps of my friend upstairs as he walks to the bathroom, the soft roar of his shower through the pipes.

When Bob comes down, I have already poured him a cup of coffee. How about a bagel? I ask like a waiter. We've got plain and New York style. I smile because Bob is originally from Brooklyn, but he picks the plain. I drop the halves into the toaster and motion him to sit at the table where I have the paper laid out. He glances at it, but decides to talk instead. "Has Ann gone already?"

"Oh, yeah. She has a class in Toledo that begins at 8:30." We both grin and shake our heads at the thought of that long pre-dawn drive. "I have margarine, butter, or cream cheese," I tell him, and he chooses butter. "I can make you an egg," I offer.

"Only if you're having one," he says. And I have to ask myself what is it I want.

"Okay, we're having an egg," I say. "How would you like it?"

"How do you usually take yours?" he asks, and I have to think again.

"I can make it anyway you'd like." I am being a real cook now.

"Over-easy then," he says as I hand him his bagel on a plate. Bob and I are the same age *fifty-five* this month, new AARP recruits, both of us losing hair and gaining weight, our kids gone off to college and beyond, both of us writers finding our way.

I scoop and turn an egg without its breaking. The other breaks and is mine. "Have you started your treatment?" he asks looking up from his plate, and I pass quickly through that curtain of fear and pain into the trust of his voice and eyes.

"Not yet," I say and explain my trip to Seattle, "It was for tests, to confirm the biopsy and to size the prostate; then they order the radiation seeds. I go back in a month." There it is out on the table, my cancer with the salt and pepper and our cups of coffee.

"Is this pretty much an experimental program?" he asks.

"Oh, no," I am quick with assurance. "It's being done all over now. But only Seattle has a record of eight years of success." It feels like the news we're discussing, but we both know it is my life and death.

"Get the best treatment," he says.

"I will, Bob." I say, and we both take a bite of bagel. There is a silence that I step through. "It's hard, you know, to talk about it with some people who don't know cancer as you do. They come up to you as you're walking down the hall and just ask how are you doing.

He nods quick, "Yeah, I know. It's like a friendly ambush."

"They tell you things, like to have it cut it out and get on with your life. One woman told me to just drink lots of juice." They say this stuff and walk away.

"We had that too, when Susan discovered her breast cancer, people meaning well but touching the wound." The dog walks past me into the kitchen.

"For a long time," I say, "I told only you and David and my brother and sisters. The hardest part was telling my children who I learned are adults. They wanted to know and to help. But I broke up on the phone each time."

"Yeah, I know. You have to take it in waves," he says. We've dealt with it a step at a time, and you can't take it to accommodate others. It's your life after all. I found one support group, Sue found another, and then the treatment and disease can change on you."

I get up and bring in the coffee pot. "It's grief," I say and he nods. "You're grieving your life. We all have to find our own way." And then face it, "I tell you, Bob. I couldn't have done it without Ann." And he nods a friend's blessing.

We eat on in thanks.

When I clean off the table, I place the dishes carefully along the sink edge and ask, "Now how about our walk?"

"Sure, I'd love it," he says, and we turn to put on our walking shoes.

*　　*　　*

We are driving down the road along the lake, and already the sun has risen. You can see blue sky and a few gulls flying over the road. At the estuary parking lot, we can hear birds off in the trees. The thermometer outside the nature center says it is 45 degrees for February. I pull the binoculars out from under the seat and say, "I once saw an eagle out here, but today we might expect to see a heron or an egret." Bob is already on the trail, so I catch up from behind.

As we enter the woods of Old Woman's Creek, we begin talking softly through patches of silence. The light breaking through bare columns of trees is a story. We listen with our eyes and hearts.

As we come to a small rise in the path, he says, "I like this place." We can see out onto the pond now, a few branches lying on thin patches of ice, the call of a heron, the screech of a gull. I have the glasses up to my eyes when I see something dark fly into the trees. We walk on ahead, and there on the wooden lookout are four older men in dark jackets with tri-pods and cameras, binoculars hanging around each of their necks. They motion us forward.

One walks up to us and whispers, "There are two eagles building a nest in the trees just to your right." I look up with the glasses as the male flies out of the nest...huge dark wings, a tail and head of white...unbelievable in the space it takes and glides through. I hand the glasses quick to Bob. Both of us know this is more than we had a right to expect. But then the fellow whispers again, "There are at least eight eagles on the pond right now. The immatures are out on the ice.... here....and here...and a pair down there in those trees. Bob turns and finds them, dark and large on the ice. He hands me the glasses, and I check out each set, forgetting to count.

We stand there mute and amazed, and soon the older men begin telling us stories of eagles. The young ones have come down from Michigan and Canada, they say. "They see the open body of water, the pair who live here, and they come down to join them." These men are part of Eagle Watchers, retired from their jobs, now early morning monitors of eagles and nests. We are six men standing together on the platform looking out across the pond and hearing tales of eagle nestings and flights. I watch the men talk in turn, a secret joy in their voices and eyes. And then I notice something; these men, who look like friends of my father, are really my age, our age, my friend Bob and me.

GETTING WORD

for Susan and Bob

My friend calls to tell me his wife has died—a week ago—so there is nothing I can do but be there on the phone with him, as he tells me how things went, how all the treatments failed, how they had to move her to a nursing home, how hospice became a blessing in the end.

"The kids are taking it well . . . considering. . ." And I hear all this deeply, words falling into a well of my own echoing, my friend's heart breaking, his voice halting, throat catching.

I tell him, "Susan was a sweet person, we will miss her too." And there is this long deep silence that only comes with parting.

He tells me friends want him to get a dog, his son takes him out to dinner now, he's back on the job after two months. "I just wanted to let you know," he tries to break it off.

"You take care of yourself," I offer back. "We're here for you," is all that's left to say.

"I know," he sighs embracing the moment, then letting go.

I go out to the kitchen where my wife and I hold each other tight, feel what all this means.

RETREAT AT WALLOON LAKE

Here in Hemingway country, northern Michigan, October leaves are falling softly onto the waters. Under blue and cloudy skies they drift then sink, Canadian Geese crossing overhead. I have come north alone for a retreat in the woods.

Last night as I fell asleep, I saw my father's face so clear before me. Dead fifteen years now, he has begun to drift from me. I no longer think of him each day, but here he was before me so real and close I could touch him. At once I felt swept and pulled by a wave—the space between us and the nearness of his life as I approach his death age. I woke to the cabin's dark, wood-grained walls, then fell back into it again. His face, so familiar, the shape and lines of him...and a tenderness rose in me for his life, this life which pains and soothes us so unpredictably–the weather of struggle and wonder.

In this threshold I waited, eyes closed, the wind blowing softly across the lake, eternal crickets outside my window. Walking back to my cabin last night, I had heard the pounding of hoofs, watched the quick blur of deer running before me into the trees. But here my father's image was clearer than any photograph and framed by light. It felt good and whole, felt deep and right. And slowly it dissolved to darkness.

I waited thinking my mother's face would next appear, but no, it was my son who rose—young man about to be a father. His quiet figure stood in a doorway portending. That week we had worked together sawing lumber for bookshelves, working steady and slowly together make things right. And I watched his hands on the wood so familiar—the hands of my father. And I stood and smiled in the knowing.

For weeks we had struggled with the project—over details outwardly, but inwardly over who was in control, who might humiliate the other. Eventually I surrendered, waited to be asked, then became the familiar gopher for my father again—holding the other end of boards, fetching the right tools, getting the light. It was no sacrifice. I had floundered for years as father, trying to pass on an ease and assurance I never had, giving him the words "I love you" that I had never heard. Work was my father's language, a brail you had to learn to read in a silence that begged understanding.

As we stood in his garage, bending over his table-saw, we felt this language of father and son. We had built something between us together. The ease and beauty of wood grain meeting wood grain. The shelves rising from the lumber and nails.

In life and dream I love those hands which rose before me— image of Smith-man holding steady at the rudder. Last night I slept deep and woke into the sound of birds.

THIS YEAR

This year my wife and I are growing an herb garden around the old bird bath–thin twists of plants beside the bricks—aroma of Italian salad everywhere.

This year Ann sleeps through the night while I rise at five to urinate, pass out some nights upon the couch, dog sleeping at my feet. "Are you okay?" we ask before coffee.

This year our children call to talk their way home through problems. Money and cars are mine, Ann listens well through pains and sorrows and dreams. Our family is extended by lovers and friends.

This year so often our work turns back into jobs as the faces in classrooms grown infinitely younger question our right to share, our ability to understand, till everything clouds with chalk dust.

This year we watch our bodies soften and round, feel old pain in necks and knees, find our hair changed each morning—brush harder on friendly teeth. Our bodies teach us patience and love.

This year we know better each other's face touched tenderly with eyes, feel the twitch in bed that says I'm already gone.

This year we hold each other tighter, breathe together through the night.

THE BRIDGE TO STEUBENVILLE

I walk out at dusk, halfway across Market Street Bridge, stare down through the steel grating to the river gliding below my feet, the light of mills spreading a film of knowing drifting through memory. A truck rolls by me disappearing into West Virginia's dark hills.

And in Ohio, streetlights of a city abandoned by the weak and monied; families huddled in living rooms, their newspaper a frozen lump in the yard.

And these gray girders near my cheek, suspended wings forged in the machines of mills, coal smoke rising in cold night air.

I have come out this night to know this—the way this river moves on, the way it remains.

RETIREMENT PLANS

I hold my retirement papers in my hands as I enter the Raddison Hotel to talk with someone from the State Teachers Retirement System. I have been fighting with them on the phone for months. Not that they would steal my money after 35 years, but rob me of my choice of when and how I would close this chapter of my life. This place is too pretty for arguing; I'm sure they count on that and on my willingness as a teacher to take instructions. They have lawyers after all, and the rules and the paperwork to prove it.

Like my father, I have given part of each paycheck to them to hold, knowing somehow they have taken and invested it elsewhere...a legitimate con, a usury of the business place. And yet they are workers too, paying into their own retirement plans, believing I suppose that they are giving me just what I deserve, the same way a young man working at Budget Car Rental double-talked me into taking insurance I already had...making money for the company so that he could move ahead into his American dream. I have taught students like him for three decades the beauty of clean prose, the honor of good work, the truth of men like Thoreau. Yet here among the palm trees and silk flowers in a world of mauve and gold, I must bargain for my retirement, prove my worth in cash paid and time served.

I am given a form to complete, pointed to a table, assigned a meeting room. And, for a long moment, I am back teaching at the high school thirty-five years ago signing in: about to step into the classroom, write my name in chalk the first time for the ten thousand students I would come to serve, struggle with, evaluate and record into the night, write notes of warning and praise. I have stood 100,000 times in the flourescent lights comparing punctuation marks with little road signs, trusted the innocence behind the eyes, the truth of their souls, the light of their questioning—the challenge and reward of those years, you say. Yes, I know all this, yet today I have come for this also: One life given over and the promise of another.

READING THE LANDSCAPE FOR THE WEATHER

"We reached inside and found that this is who we really are."
                                        -Sioux City, Iowa, resident

Last night my wife and I watched the story of Flight 232, the DC 10 whose tail engine exploded on July 19th in 1989, causing the plane to lose control for 45 minutes, then crash into a cornfield by the runway at Sioux City, Iowa. Again and again we watched the fiery wings flop over in slow motion as the plane disappeared into a black cloud of smoke.

No one thought they could bring it in; no one expected any would survive.

A week later when the pilot watched the film from his hospital bed, he cried aloud. "Oh, my God! Where was that? No one could have survived!" The stewardess found herself hanging from her seat as a flash of flames swept through the fuselage; slowly she dropped down and walked out into an Iowa cornfield, then turned to hold back the torn shards of metal as others walked out into evening sunlight and the arms of Iowa rescuers.

185 survived. 110 did not. All were changed forever.

It's a story that pounds in your heart. But what held me most was those 45 minutes of doomed flight as rudderless they circled aimlessly right. Into the silence came gasps of pain, whimpers of fear, and the hush of prayer as they held themselves together. In the final moments they leaned forward to the floor that would soon explode. One woman coached herself, "You're going to make it. You're going to do it. You will survive." Others cried softly and said their last goodbyes. One man just wanted the waiting to end. "For Christ's sake, let it come."

Below in the flight tower, the air controller had twice given up though his voice continued to assure the commander. "You are nearing the runway. Your altitude is good. Your speed is excessive." There was no way to slow it down.

110 died. 184 survived. All were changed forever.

Ground crews watched the plane disappear into its own flames and smoke. "It seemed to disintegrate," they said, as they rushed towards its remains only to see a man walking towards them dazed. "In that instant," another said, "our whole mission was changed."

And this is the part I can hardly explain.

As we watched and heard all this, I felt this time the solid kinship of survivors, those who have faced doom and despair and risen, those who have endured the minutes or hours, the months or years, and survived, though others have surely died and though wounds clearly remain. This time holding my wife's soft hand, I too was walking from the ashes and rubble, out the torn metal hulk and past the lush green cornstalks where I stood with them in life's clear light and open air.

THE AFTERMATH
(September 2001)

That morning the planes came slashing the heart of America, right before our eyes, burning and tumbling buildings full of people— Good god! That day I felt such devastation I cried inside, "They've spoiled everything..." meaning our hopes for this world. The pain came into my body then in a shock wave so strong I could only ache, not cry. And we all carried it with us in our eyes, our voices full of grief, trying to remain calm in the face of such murderous hate.

I let my students talk of it, absorbed some of their pain and rage, naming our emotions as in meditation, seeking to know, release, and go on. But it wasn't until we watched the rescuers climbing among the smoke and rubble that we knew somehow we could go on with courage caring for each other.

Then one morning Ann and I decided to send our healing intentions to those who grieved and those who were taken in mid-breath or leading others away from the wreckage. Call it a prayer or a silent healing wave of energy, we sent it out and felt it move within. We began again the grounding of our spirits in our caring for our world. Some sent food and clothes and money, others gave blood and time and labor. It became a wave pushing back the terror of blinding hatred that had been forced onto our lives. We too rose from the broken rubble with clear intent.

For weeks I had been unable to read or write, and then one afternoon I turned off the television and sat with the pain in stillness till someone knocked and the door came open with my grandson running happily toward me and eager to feed the birds in the yard.

I will not write the poem of the War on America.
I will not speak the pain we all have taken in
a hundred times, feeling the dark planes slash through
100, 000, 000 lives, severing reason from the brain.
Someone else will write those poems, I am sure.

Watching the faces of the young, I pray for a brave wisdom.
For if intention can so disrupt, it can also re-connect.
And so I write of the wounded faces filled with care,
the tired hands reaching others, pulling them to safety there,
of those holding photos who wait in rain.

I would write instead the poem of sweet intention
inside my grandson's eyes reading the wild geese
across the skies, long after they have gone,
of my own wife's turning to hold me close,
my saying, "We'll get through this" one more time
and believing it, as I do the rain.

THE SPIRAL WALK

I take the path into the woods knowing that darkness is falling and all about me the songs are rising—Nature eternal and my own—echoing.

Out in the pond stands a great blue heron—steely gray in the silver light of dusk where the moon coming up meets the sun going down.

And it is not the bird of Nature books nor the one of mythic poems. The blue heron standing in moonlit water is the blue heron standing in moonlit water. And the one watching from shore is the one watching from shore.

I cannot hold this moment any longer than itself, and it passes through me: water in my hands / the air around me. I must let go, go back into the town, my house, the lights, my life where phones ring, and the dog needs let out.

I taste this hunger and sorrow, this joy and trust, knowing the risk of loss and the truth that only comes by touching all that I am, the heart open to itself.

APRIL

for Ann

Though this path is unfamiliar, I will remember it always and the cool rush of spring wind across the lake.

Black grackles in the thick branched sky as we walk wordless under early sun.

And the light is a wave of lilac reminding us of home, our warm bed, the way the world begins and ends.

(photo: Kat Neyberg)

Larry Smith is a native of the industrial Ohio River Valley, born in Mingo Junction, Ohio, in 1943. He is a graduate of Mingo Central High School, Muskingum College, and Kent State University. Smith has worked as a steel mill laborer, a high school English teacher, and as a professor of English and Humantities at Firelands College of Bowling Green State University.

A writer, editor, publisher, Smith directs the Firelands Writing Center of Firelands College and Bottom Dog Press, an independent small press. His recent books include: *Working It Out* (novel) Ridgeway Press, 1997; *Kenneth Patchen: Rebel Poet in America* (biography) Small Press Consortium 1999; *Chinese Zen Poems,* trans. with Mei Hui Huang, Bottom Dog Press 1996; *Thoreau's Lost Journal* (poems) Westron Press 2001. He and filmmaker Tom Koba co-produced two video docudramas: *James Wright's Ohio* and *Kenneth Patchen: An Art of Engagement.*

His essays, reviews, and articles have appeared widely. He and his wife Ann, an associate professor of nursing, are the parents of three adult children. They live along Lake Erie in Huron, Ohio.